OPEN ROAD'S BEST OF

Southern
California

by Elizabeth Borsting

**Open Road Travel Guides – designed for the
amount of time you *really* have for your trip!**

Open Road Publishing

Open Road's new travel guides.
Designed to cut to the chase.
You don't need a huge travel encyclopedia – you need a *selective guide*
to steer you right. If you're going on vacation for a few weeks or less,
get a guide that brings you the *best* of any destination for the amount
of time you *really* have for your trip!

Open Road – the guide you need for the trip you want.

The New Open Road *Best Of* Travel Guides.
Right to the point.
Uncluttered.
Easy.

To My Favorite Travel Companions: Kurt, Jake, Katie and Ruby Jean

Open Road Publishing
P.O. Box 284, Cold Spring Harbor, NY 11724
www.openroadguides.com

Text Copyright © 2007 by Elizabeth A. Borsting
- All Rights Reserved -
ISBN 1-59360-094-1
Library of Congress Control No. 2006940246

About the Author
Elizabeth Arrighi Borsting is a freelance writer and public relations consultant
for the hospitality industry. Her writing credits include *Celebrity Weddings &*
Honeymoon Getaways, Open Road's Southern California Guide, California's Best
B&Bs, and *LA With Kids*. She served as a contributing editor for both *Honeymoon*
Magazine and *Preferred Destinations*. Her work has also appeared in the *Los*
Angeles Times and *National Geographic Traveler*. She resides with her husband
Kurt and their two children, Jake and Katie, plus pup Ruby Jean along the coast
in Long Beach, California, just south of Los Angeles.

CONTENTS

Your Passport to the **Perfect Trip!**

Maps

PHOTO CREDITS

1. INTRODUCTION

From San Diego to Santa Barbara, the desert to the sea, **Southern California** offers a wealth of great vacation choices. And this is *the* go-to guide for your trip. You'll find exactly what you need to help plan an effortless holiday. What you *won't* find is a clutter of unnecessary options, as we've taken a *less is more* approach. We've done the work for you!

Athletes and sporty types can surf, golf, play tennis, and participate in a game of beach volleyball. If historic sites and landmarks are more to your liking, you can visit plenty of those places too, from historic lighthouses and beacons along the coast to some of the original 18th-century missions established by Father Junipero Serra. You can also go behind the scenes on the backlot of a movie studio, enjoy a photo-op below the famed Hollywood Sign, and visit the places where Tinseltown's top celebrities hang out.

I've selected plush resorts, great spas and terrific restaurants. If your plans call for a stay at a five-star waterfront resort, you'll find only the finest have made the cut. If you prefer a more understated and elegant inn, those are listed too. You'll dine on meals prepared by a celebrity chef one night, and pony up to the deli counter at a century-old restaurant the next to order a classic French dip sandwich served on a sturdy paper plate. As for attractions, all the usual suspects are here—Disneyland, Knott's Berry Farm, Universal Studios, SeaWorld, and LEGOland—along with others that you're likely unaware of.

So get packing – the *best* is yet to come!

2. OVERVIEW

You may feel as if you're already familiar with Southern California. After all, the region has served as the backdrop for countless television shows, movie productions, award presentations and, dare we say, real life dramas. It's almost as if the rest of the world has come to know Southern California through the technology of satellites, celluloid, Internet surfing and tabloid journalism.

But art — and the evening news — don't always imitate life, at least accurately. There is so much more to Southern California than

 just sandy beaches, expensive cars, designer labels, and yards of red carpets. The region is more complex and multifaceted than anything the silver screen could capture. Yes, the movie industry produces a ripple effect up and down the coast, and its presence plays an instrumental role in helping to shape both the economy and trends. But sometimes Hollywood takes on a supporting role to some of the region's other star attractions.

To help make your planning as effortless as possible, this book has been sectioned into five different destinations. This chapter will briefly describe each of the regions and include a few, brief itineraries to help you make the most of your trip.

Los Angeles
With a metropolitan area more than twice the size of Switzerland, Los Angeles County can boggle the mind. You may be amazed to learn that seven regions fit snugly within the confines of the

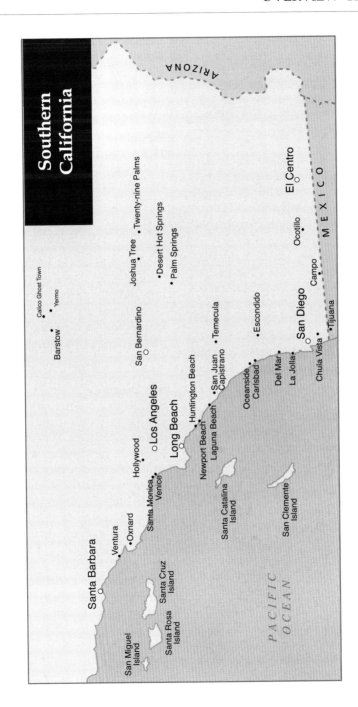

Southern California

Worth Planning Your Trip Around ...

- A night at the **Holly-wood Bowl** in Los Angeles, May-September
- The **Santa Barbara Vintners' Festival**, April
- The annual **Julian Apple Harvest** in North San Diego County, September-November
- A Polo Match at the **Will Rogers Polo Club** in Los Angeles, May-September
- **Pageant of the Masters** in Laguna Beach, July-August
- Newport Beach's **Christmas Boat Parade**, December
- The **Bob Hope PGA Chrysler Classic** in Rancho Mirage, January
- **San Diego's Street Scene** in the Gaslamp Quarter, September
- The New Year's Day **Tournament of Roses Parade** in Pasadena, January
- **Fiesta Days** in Downtown Santa Barbara, August

county line. But you don't have time to see all those regions nor would you want to. I've only included those that truly have something to offer including **Downtown Los Angeles, Pasadena, West Hollywood, Beverly Hills, Hollywood, West Los Angeles**, and the **coastal communities**.

Los Angeles, and its environs, has something for everyone. There's museums, historic buildings, architectural offerings, fabulous shopping, the beaches, some of the world's best hotels and restaurants, and, of course, the glamour of Hollywood.

San Diego

San Diego is our nation's seventh largest city and the birthplace of California. The county begins at the Mexican border and abuts the southern tip of Orange County, which is more than 70 miles to the north. As large as it is, San Diego still manages to evoke a small-town feel, yet with **Mexico** just minutes away, you'll discover a distinct international flair. Much of the action takes place in and around downtown San Diego and its harbor area, as well as Coronado Island and the nearby beaches. San Diego's coastal resort towns and a few of its main attractions are found in the north county region.

Orange County

There was little fanfare among the thousands of orange groves prior to the 1955 opening of **Disneyland**. But the popularity of the theme park, coupled with several miles of **pristine coastline** and **fabulous shopping venues**, has propelled Orange County into one of Southern California's main destinations. The county features some charming seaside communities, fabulous waterfront resorts, and its own presidential library.

Santa Barbara

Fondly called the American Riviera, the town of Santa Barbara is a charming seaside community. It's rich history of Spanish and Mexican influences are evident in its downtown architectural nuances, where buildings are graced with red-tiled roofs, arched entryways, hidden courtyard and ornate fountains.

There is much to see and do in Santa Barbara, yet there is never the feeling of haste. You won't find commercial theme parks, monstrous shopping malls or fabricated walking districts. Instead, you'll discover plenty one-of-a-kind boutiques and sidewalk cafes up and down **State Street**, the town's main thoroughfare, as well as historic adobe structures, manicured public gardens and plump, vine-ripened grapes along bucolic trails ready to be pressed for wine.

Palm Springs

Palm Springs and the neighboring Desert Resort Communities provide the setting for the quintessential weekend getaway. There are several very different influences that make the area so unique. Native American tribes own and operate the fun, Vegas-style casinos, while the powers of Hollywood are felt at the luxe resorts and annual film festival.

The desert is a favorite year-round destination for gay and lesbian travelers, and you'll find many hotels and resorts that specialize in this niche market. Aside from lounging poolside, playing golf or tennis, or draping yourself across a massage table, you'll find unique and unexpected attractions beneath the desert sun.

Itineraries
If you've never been to Southern California, you'll want to be sure to take in the highlights, those "must-see" and landmarks. If all you can spare is a weekend, choose an area and concentrate on the attractions in and around that destination.

Great places for a weekend jaunt include:
• Downtown LA and Hollywood
• Santa Monica and Venice
• Coastal Orange County
• Disneyland Resort
• Downtown San Diego and Mission/Pacific Beach
• North County San Diego
• Downtown Santa Barbara and the Wine Country
• Palm Springs

10 Don't-Miss Ideas ...

• Enjoy a **Gourmet Picnic** at a Santa Barbara Winery
• Pamper yourself with a **spa treatment** at a luxe Palm Springs resort
• Star gaze at **Griffith Observatory** in Los Angeles
• Slumber in an **oceanfront room** along the Orange County Coast
• Spend the night at the **Hotel Del Coronado** in San Diego
• Visit **Catalina Island**
• Have a **nighttime bonfire** at Bolsa Chica State Beach in Orange County
• Visit the **Forecourt of the Stars** in front of Grauman's Chinese Theatre, and compare your hand and footprints to famous Hollywood icons
• Savor a sunset cocktail at the **Top of the Hyatt**—40 floors up—at the Manchester Grand Hyatt in Downtown San Diego
• **Hand-feed Baringo giraffes**, including the one with the crooked neck, at the Santa Barbara Zoo

If you have an entire week to spend, you can fit in two regions, maybe three at the most.

Itineraries for a One-Week Holiday in Southern California:
• Santa Barbara
• LA and Santa Barbara
• LA and Orange County
• Orange County and San Diego
• Palm Springs with up to 2 additional destinations: San Diego, Orange County *or* LA
• LA, Orange County and San Diego

Don't try to experience the entire region in a single week, as it's impossible. By doing so, you would have to spend an average of one night in each destination, then account for several hours spent driving to each location; when you factor in these elements, in the end you really won't have accomplished much.

Each destination chapter of this book guides you to the best sights in that region. Only you can decide what really piques your interest. So, take a look at what is presented, then earmark those venues that sound the most appealing, and create your very own custom-made itinerary.

3. LOS ANGELES

Los Angeles. City of Angeles. La La Land. Call it what you like, Los Angeles is a town like no other. With its pretzel-like freeway connections, towering skyline and sophisti-cated allure, it remains one of the world's largest and most influential metropolises. Los Angeles is a mosaic of many styles, influences and cultures. It's a vast and sprawling region comprised of many individual communities, includ-ing **Downtown Los Angeles, Hollywood, West Holly-wood, Beverly Hills,** and **Santa Monica** along the coast.

There is literally something for everyone within the city limits and beyond. Urban resorts and hip restaurants cater to both the curious traveler and Hollywood moguls. Muse-ums and theme parks abound. Landmarks, such as the infamous Hollywood Sign and Grauman's Chinese The-atre, offer exciting photo opportunities. And even some of the more mundane tasks of every day life, like a trip to the grocery store, can result in a brush with fame.

ONE GREAT DAY IN L.A.

Got only hours to spare? Not to worry; it's possible to take in the highlights and still feel like you got a taste of L.A. Begin the morning in downtown at the Flower Market and Olvera Street before proceeding west towards Hollywood where you'll stroll through the **Farmers Market** on Fairfax, then hop on the faux trolley to the nearby **Grove**. Wander **Hollywood Boulevard** taking in the all the famous sights: the **Walk of Fame**, **Hollywood Roosevelt Hotel**, **Grauman's Chinese Theatre** and its **Forecourt of the Stars**. End the evening at an old Hollywood haunt, **Musso and Frank's**, known for its roomy banquettes and oversized martinis, and a movie at the **ArcLight Cinema**.

Haul yourself out of bed early and start your day in Downtown Los Angeles at the **Flower Mart**, which opens at 2am to the trade and wholesale market and at 8am to the public. This is the West Coast's largest floral supplier, and there is an abundant of energy and aromas as florists from all over comb through the hundreds of blooms. *Info:* www.laflowerdistrict.com. Tel. 213/622-3696. Downtown. 766 Wall Street. Free.

After you leave the Flower Mart, head to **The Pantry** *(see Los Angeles Sleeps & Eats)* at Figueroa and 9th Street. This is an L.A. landmark that has been opened 24 hours a day, seven days a week for nearly eight decades. Currently Richard Riordan, the former Mayor of Los Angeles, owns the restaurant. The Pantry is small with a few tables and counter service; coffee is included with each meal. The menu is no-frills: eggs, bacon, sausage, pancakes, steak and potatoes. The sourdough toast is thick, buttered and grilled. There's always a line out the door, so expect a wait. There is a separate line for counter service, which usually moves much quicker.

After breakfast, you'll want to visit some of downtown's landmarks and architectural treasures. **El Pueblo de Los Angeles State Historic Park** is where Los Angeles really began when the first pueblo was established here in 1781 under the rule of Spain. In 1930, many of the buildings were saved from demolition by establishing the area as a Mexican-style marketplace known as Olvera Street. Some notable structures along the esplanade include the **1818 Avila Adobe**, the **Pelaconi House**, the city's oldest brick house dating back to 1855, and the **1877 Sepulveda House**, an Eastlake Victorian-style structure. There are shops, restaurants and vendor carts that also line the pathway. *Info:* www.olvera-street.com. Tel. 213/628-1274. Downtown. 849 N. Alameda St. Open Daily 10am-70pm; some stores and restaurants may stay open later. Free.

From Olvera Street, cross Alameda Street and head to **Union Station**, the last of America's magnificent train depots built in 1939. The Spanish Colonial Revival structure is blended with streamline touches reflecting the Art Deco era in which it was built. The soaring clock tower and arched entryways are complemented with a landscape of fig trees, Mexican fan palms, and birds of paradise. These days, Union Station is bustling with local commuters and passengers from afar. It is also a favorite backdrop for location scouts and has been featured in countless films, including *LA Confidential, Speed, Pearl Harbor, Blade Runner,* and many other notable and forgettable films. *Info:* Tel. 800/872-7245. Downtown.

If it's lunchtime, don't leave downtown without first stopping into **Philippe, The Original** *(see Los Angeles Best Sleeps & Eats)* at the corner of Alameda and Ord near Union Station and Olvera Street. Opened since 1908, this is where the French dip sandwich was invented.

From Philippe's, drive west on Sunset Boulevard towards Hollywood. At Fairfax, you'll turn left and cruise down towards **Farmers Market**. A true farmers market actually originated here in 1934 with farmers displaying their wares in a dirt parking lot at the corner of Third and Fairfax. Eventually wood stalls were erected, along with the landmark clock tower, both of which still

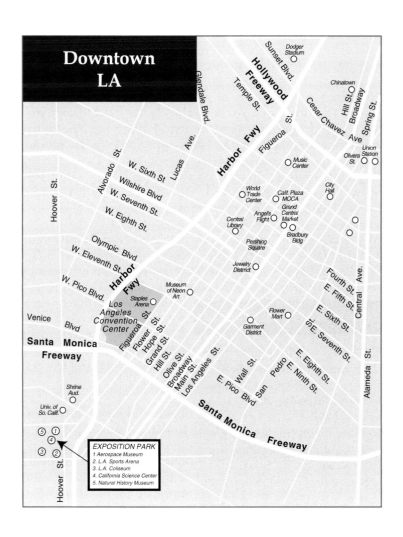

Downtown LA

Dodger Stadium

Sunset Blvd.

Hollywood Freeway

Temple St.

Chinatown

Hill St.

Broadway

Spring St.

Glendale Blvd.

Cesar Chavez Ave

Harbor Fwy

Figueroa St.

Union Station

Olivera St.

Alvorado St.

W. Sixth St

Lucas Ave.

Music Center

City Hall

Wilshire Blvd

W. Seventh St.

Hoover St.

W. Eighth St.

World Trade Center

Calif. Plaza MOCA

Central Library

Angel's Flight

Grand Central Market

Bradbury Bldg

Pershing Square

Olympic Blvd

W. Eleventh St

Jewelry District

W. Pico Blvd.

Harbor Fwy

Museum of Neon Art

Fourth St.

E. Fifth St.

Central Ave.

Venice Blvd

Staples Arena

Los Angeles Convention Center

Figueroa St.

Flower St.

Hope St.

Grand St.

Olive St.

Hill St.

Broadway

Main St.

Los Angeles St.

Flower Mart

E. Sixth St.

Garment District

E. Seventh St.

E. Eighth St.

Wall St.

San Pedro

E. Ninth St.

Alameda St.

Santa Monica Freeway

E. Pico Blvd

Shrine Aud.

Univ. of So. Calif.

Santa Monica Freeway

Hoover St.

⑤ ①
④
③ ②

EXPOSITION PARK
1 Aerospace Museum
2. L.A. Sports Arena
3. L.A. Coliseum
4. California Science Center
5. Natural History Museum

exist today. Farmers Market has become a rather happening place to be of late with plenty of restaurant stalls and a few full-service eateries. You'll find everything from gumbo to crepes to a fromagerie. Celebrities, such as Denzel Washington and Jennifer Aniston, are known to take in the scenery along with everyone else. There are also shops; the fruit and vegetable stands still exist. *Info:* www.farmersmarketla.com. Tel. 323/933-9211. Fairfax District. Corner of 3rd and Fairfax.

From Farmers Market you can walk along the cobblestone pathway to **The Grove** or take the double-decker, track-driven trolley, which operates between the two destinations. The Grove, which resembles a European town square, is LA's newest outdoor lifestyle and entertainment center punctuated with dancing fountains, bridges, upscale stores, and sidewalk cafes. *Info:* www.thegrovela.com. Tel. 888/315-8883. Fairfax District. Corner of 3rd and Fairfax next to the Farmers Market.

After leaving The Grove, head north to the corner of **Hollywood and Highland**, a lifestyle center named for its location at Hollywood and Highland. This intersection offers the quintessential Hollywood experience with **Grauman's Chinese Theatre** and its **Forecourt of the Stars**, where you can compare your hand and footprints to celebrities past and present who have had their hands and feet cast in cement.

Grauman's "Footnote"

The first cement impressions at **Grauman's Chinese Theater** were accidentally left by actress **Norma Talmadge**, who stepped into a block of wet cement at the theater's forecourt. Always one to seize an opportunity, Sid Grauman quickly masked the faux pas by insisting the actress sign her name in the cement. The tradition took hold when Mary Pickford and Douglas Fairbanks repeated the gimmick a few weeks later on April 30, 1927.

Take a guided tour of the **Kodak Theatre,** home of the annual Academy Awards ceremony. Tours depart every half hour from the Level 2 entrance and last approximately 30 minutes, just enough time to see an Oscar statuette, find out what seats celebrities occupied during the most recent Academy Awards presentation, pay a visit to the George Eastman VIP Room and other exclusive celebrity hot spots, and view images from previous awards ceremonies. *Info:* www.kodaktheatre.com. Tel. 323/308-6300. Hollywood. Corner of Hollywood & Highland. Tours are $15 adults, $10 children.

Afterwards, stroll the **Hollywood Walk of Fame** along Hollywood Boulevard where more than 2,000 terrazzo stars grace the sidewalk in a display of celebrity adoration. The star-studded sidewalks cover

ALTERNATIVE PLAN
Not a big fan of Hollywood lore? Then take a guided **Red Line Tour of Downtown LA.** These walking excursions, conducted by expert guides, take you inside such landmarks as the Grand Central Market, Edison Building, Central Library, the historic Biltmore Hotel, the Palace and Orpheum Theatres, Clifton's Cafeteria, and the Warner Pantages Theatre. *Info:* Tel. 323/402-1074. Afterwards, pay a visit to the **George C. Page Museum** and famed **La Brea Tar Pits,** the **Los Angeles County Museum of Modern Art,** or the **Peterson Automotive Museum.** You can also sleuth around some of the city's unique neighborhoods, including **Little Ethiopia, Thai Town, Melrose Avenue** or **Westwood,** where the campus of UCLA is located.

18 blocks east to west along both sides of Hollywood Boulevard, from Gower to La Brea, and three blocks north and south along Vine Street from Sunset to Yucca.

Next head over to the nearby **Hollywood Museum** located inside the historic **Max Factor Building.** This is a film aficionado's paradise featuring a collection of movie artifacts and memorabilia, including costumes from celebrated films, Sylvester Stallone's boxing gloves from the movie

Rocky, Cary Grant's Rolls Royce, and many other relics. *Info:* www.thehollywoodmusuem.com. Tel. 323/464-7776. Hollywood. 1660 N. Highland Avenue. Open Thu-Sun 10am-5pm. Admission is $15 adults, $12 children.

Since the **Hollywood Museum** pays homage to many Tinseltown legends, it seems only fitting to head east on Hollywood Boulevard to the legendary **Musso & Frank's**. The restaurant, located near Hollywood & Vine, was established in 1919 and has long been a favorite watering hole of the stars*(see Los Angeles Sleeps & Eats)*.

Finish up the evening by taking a short drive south on Vine towards Sunset Boulevard. Near the corner of Sunset and Vine is the **ArcLight Cinemas**, a unique theater complex featuring a café with a full menu of California cuisine plus a balcony bar, where film buffs can watch a movie while enjoying their favorite alcoholic beverages. The futuristic geodesic **Cinerama Dome**, built in 1963, was refurbished in recent years and is *the* place in Los Angeles to see a movie. The Arclight has an all-reserved seating policy that allows you to choose your specific seat. *Info:* www.arclightcinemas.com. 6360 Sunset Boulevard. Hollywood. Tel. 323/464-4226.

A FANTASTIC L.A. WEEKEND

Nothing is more fantastic than 72 hours spent near the beach. Think palm trees, the sound of pounding surf, and a few great diversions all packed into a single weekend. Throw some sunshine into the mix and moonlit evenings, and you've just described the quintessential L.A. weekend.

Friday Evening
Check in to **Shutters Hotel on the Beach** (*see Los Angeles Best Sleeps & Eats*) then check out the view from your balcony. The hotel, built in 1993, is reminiscent of a vintage beach resort but with all the luxuries needed for a fabulous 48-hour escape. After you've settled in, enjoy your surroundings at **The Lobby Lounge** inside the hotel. This is a great spot for a celebratory cocktail or light meal, and a prime spot for people watching.

While there is still time, take a stroll along **Ocean Avenue** towards the historic **Santa Monica Pier**, whose entrance is marked by a vintage neon sign announcing the destination. As you descend down towards the pier, to your left is the famed 1916 **Santa Monica Carousel**. Take a whirl on this classic merry-go-round, which is still a bargain at just 50 cents a spin. The  classic Looff-designed carousel, housed inside a hippodrome building, has been featured in countless movies, including *The Sting*, *Forrest Gump* and *Ruthless People*, to name a few. More thrills await at the end of the pier at **Pacific Park**, featuring a nine-story, solar powered Ferris wheel and thrilling roller coaster.

After you've strolled the pier, head back towards Ocean Avenue. At the entrance to the pier is **The Lobster**, offering great seafood and some of the best ocean views. Ask to be seated on the outside deck, order an ample-sized martini, and drink in the view. Afterwards, you can check out the scene along **Third Street Promenade** where there are plenty of shops, more restaurants and bars, bookstores, and a lively street scene, or return to your room and savor the ocean views from your balcony.

Saturday
Without a doubt, you'll want to start the morning with a leisurely stroll along **Santa Monica's strand**. The paved pathway is bustling with joggers, cyclists and walkers. After walking you'll want to have a little breakfast back at your hotel inside **Pedals**, which looks out onto the strand. Afterwards, check out the flavors at the **Farmers' Market** along Arizona Avenue at Third Street featuring fresh fruit and vegetable stands, flower stalls, and other organic treats.

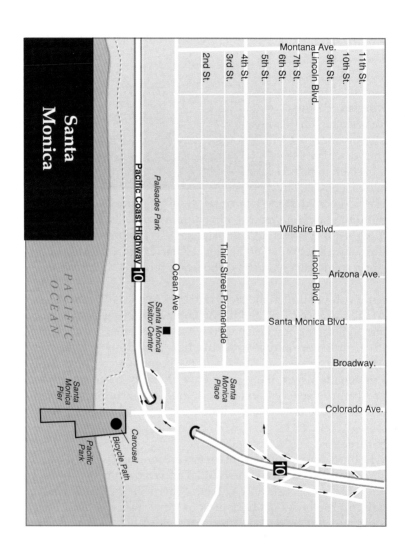

Now hop in the car and head to the chic shops along **Montana Avenue**, located at the northern edge of town. This hip stretch of boutiques and eateries includes 10 blocks of top-quality clothing, home furnishings, accessories and gifts punctuated with bistros, cafes, and bakeries. **Governor Arnold Schwarzenegger** and wife **Maria Shriver** are often spotted here, as are tons of other celebrities. You'll grab lunch at **Father's Office**, a local and celebrated Montana Avenue pub serving great burgers and sandwiches.

When you've had enough, get back in the car (LA *is* a driving town, after all) and carve out the rest of the day for **The Getty Center**. Situated atop a terraced hillside and designed by renowned architect Richard Meier, this is LA's premiere museum. Be sure to visit the Central Garden, hidden from view, where you

can relax among the trees, fountains, and reflecting pools between gallery hopping. In addition to rotating exhibitions, The Getty Center houses a collection of pre-20th-century European paintings, drawings, illuminated manuscripts, sculpture, decorative art and photographs with selected works by such artists as van Gogh, Renoir and Cezzane. If you have small children in tow, check out the **Family Room** with its hands-on activities, games and displays. *Info:* www.thegetty.edu/visit. Tel. 310/440-7300. Brentwood. 1200 Getty Center Drive. Open Tuesday-Thursday and Sunday 10am-6pm, Friday and Saturday 10am-9pm. Free admission. $8 to park.

You'll likely have quite an appetite once you're through walking around the multi-acre Getty Center. Make your way back to the car and head east on Sunset Boulevard towards Hollywood, where you'll dine at **Yamashiro Restaurant** at 1999 N. Sycamore (*see Los Angeles Best Sleeps & Eats*), high above Hollywood Boulevard. After dinner, and in keeping with the Far East architectural theme, wander down to Hollywood Boulevard and catch a movie at **Grauman's Chinese Theatre**.

ALTERNATIVE PLAN
If Cal-Asian food isn't to your liking, then skip dinner at Yamashiro and make that your final stop for an after-dinner drink. Instead, dine at another Hollywood landmark – **Miceli's** *(see Los Angeles Best Sleeps & Eats)*. Opened in 1949, this no-frills restaurant serves excellent pasta, pizza, veal and seafood in the heart of Hollywood.

If there's nothing playing that's worthwhile, then get in the car and make your way to the **Beverly Hills Hotel** *(see Los Angeles Best Sleeps & Eats)* on Sunset Boulevard for a nightcap at the very celebrity-laden **Polo Lounge**. Don't miss an opportunity to walk the grounds and take a peek at the infamous pool, where many a Hollywood deal have been brokered. Then simply take the original long and winding road — **Sunset Boulevard** — south where it ends at Pacific Coast Highway. Hang a left and head back towards Santa Monica.

Sunday
Begin your morning with a drive up Pacific Coast Highway towards Malibu. Stop at **Duke's Malibu**, 21150 Pacific Coast Highway *(see Los Angeles Best Sleeps & Eats)* for Sunday brunch, making sure to snag a window table on the enclosed oceanfront patio. Afterwards, get back in the car heading towards Santa Monica and continue on to Venice Beach, known mainly for its fun and funky boardwalk. The boardwalk is a virtual circus sideshow with some outrageous street entertainment strung out along **Ocean Front Walk**. The strand is also dotted with sidewalk

cafes, street vendors hawking their wares, souvenir and t-shirt shops. There are also basketball and handball courts, and **Muscle Beach** is where all the bodybuilders flex their muscles while pumping iron in front of passersby. Arnold Schwarzenegger was a regular here during the 1970s, long before he embarked on a movie or political career.

Once you've had enough of the freak show, turn your attention to **Beyond Baroque** (www.beyondbaroque.com. Tel. 310/822-3006. 681 Venice Boulevard), a literary arts center located in the Old City Hall. The center hosts several literary events a month and boasts a fascinating bookstore. From there, head to **Abbot Kinney Boulevard**, an emerging area known for its unique shops, coffeehouses, and bistros. The street is named for Venice's founder, Abbot Kinney, who modeled this seaside community after Venice, Italy, and gave this city one of its greatest gifts: **The Venice Canals**. Located between Washington and Venice at Dell, you'll park the car and walk about to view some of the beautiful homes, some of which belong to celebrities.

After you've strolled along the canals, get back in the car and head to Santa Monica's **Main Street** for dinner. Located just a few blocks from the beach, this is where the locals tend to gravitate. There are a number of nice restaurants, including Wolfgang Puck's **Chinois on Main** and **The Library Alehouse**, an upscale pub with patio dining.

A WONDERFUL WEEK IN L.A.

With an entire week to spend in Los Angeles, you'll have a chance to see many of the highlights. You'll prowl some prestigious museums and landmarks, take a tour of a **movie studio**, go for a serene hike in the **Hollywood Hills**, scream your head off at a **theme park** and, who knows, maybe you'll even bump into a celebrity along the way.

RECOMMENDED PLAN: One thing you'll discover quickly is just how sprawling Los Angeles is. You really can't maneuver about without a vehicle. Spend a day in and around **Downtown Los Angeles**, another day on the **Westside** (Beverly Hills, West Hollywood, Hollywood), and a day at **Universal Studios** (or Disneyland in neighboring Orange County). Set aside some time to hang out at one of the beach cities, take a drive from one end of

Sunset Boulevard to the other, and visit **Old Town Pasadena**, home of the Tournament of Roses Parade. Don't forget to set aside a day to visit one of LA's extraordinary museums.

Downtown Los Angeles
See map on page 19.

Downtown Los Angeles is in the midst of a renaissance. Old, abandoned buildings are enjoying a new lease on life as hip, residential lofts. There are new restaurants and developments, including LA Live, a lifestyle complex currently being developed near STAPLES Center.

Don't Miss ...

- **Griffith Observatory** and its views of the LA Basin
- **The Getty Center**, LA's premiere museum
- **Hollywood Forever Cemetery**, the final resting place for Hollywood legends
- shopping at **The Grove & Farmers Market**
- a summer evening at the **Hollywood Bowl**
- **Forecourt of the Stars** at Grauman's Chinese Theatre
- a stroll down **Rodeo Drive**
- **Olvera Street**, the birthplace of LA

Begin your day in the **Fashion District**, formerly known as the Garment District, where you'll find fabulous deals on designer clothes and, more likely, knock-offs. There are some 1,000 stores that sell to the general public at heavily discounted prices – expect to save 30-70 percent off retail. Independent retailers line the streets and alleys with no national retailers to be found. The upside to shopping here is that many of the owners are willing to bargain, offering even a greater discount on name brands than what the price tag indicates.

After you've had your fill of shopping, head to **Exposition Park**, located across the street from the **University of Southern California** (USC) near Downtown LA at the confluence of Figueroa and Jefferson Boulevard. The 25-acre site dates back to 1872 when it was used as an agricultural fairground. The 1932

Summer Olympics were held at the **Memorial Coliseum,** which was also the site of the 1984 Summer Olympics as well as the 1959 World Series and a pair of NFL Super Bowl games. Here, in the middle of Los Angeles, is the fabulous **Rose Garden,** fragrant and free to the public, this urban utopia offers 150 varieties of the delicate bloom and is punctuated with gazebos and fountains. Within a petal-toss is the **Natural History Museum of LA County,** housed in a 1913 Spanish Revival building. Take some time to explore the layout of exhibits that detail the earth's evolution starting some 4.5 billion years ago. *Info:* www.nhm.org. Tel. 213/763-DINO. Open 9:30am-5pm Monday-Friday, and 10am-5pm on weekends and holidays. Admission is $9 adults, $6.50 students. Next-door is the **California Science Center** where admission is free. The museum prides itself on displays that are interactive and hands-on. Across the way is the Frank Gehry-designed **IMAX** Theater measuring seven stories high and 90-feet wide. The theater features revolving topics and offers shows daily. *Info:* www.californiasciencecenter.org. Tel. 213/744-7400. Open daily 10am-5pm. Admission is $8 adults, $4.75 children.

ALTERNATIVE PLAN
If you're not much of a shopper, then skip the Fashion District and visit two of downtown's newest architectural and cultural treasures. Tour the **Cathedral of Our Lady of the Angels** in downtown. Free tours of the cathedral are available Monday-Friday at 1pm. You'll walk through the grounds, get a detailed look at the priceless artwork, and get an overview of the 11-story structure and its magnificent architecture. *Info:* www.olacathedral.org. Tel. 213/680-5200. 555 West Temple Street. Then visit the gleaming Frank Gehry-designed **Walt Disney Concert Hall**. The 90-minute tour includes the original three venues and the lobby of the concert hall. Tours are available daily as performance schedules permit. Then enjoy lunch at the Concert Hall Café. *Info:* www.musiccenter.org. Tel. 213/972-7211. Corner of 1st and Hope Streets. Guided tours: $8 per person.

Head to **Griffith Park** to visit the 75-acre **Los Angeles Zoo**. Here you'll find more than 2,000 animals residing with or near other animals from their original continent. In addition to mammals, birds and reptiles, the zoo also houses invertebrates, such as exotic cockroaches, scorpions, and black widow spiders. A trip to the Animal Nursery is where the newest arrivals are kept. You can picnic in the park, and there are also tram tours. *Info:* www.lazoo.org. Tel. 323/644-4200. Griffith's Park. 5333 Zoo Drive. Open daily 10am-5pm. Admission $10 adults, $5 children.

Just west of downtown is the **Mid-Wilshire District**, a roughly one-mile stretch between Fairfax and La Brea Avenues. Known as Miracle Mile or Museum Row, the area once housed many of LA's upscale department stores. Many of the streamlined, Art Deco buildings from the area's heyday remain. The Page Museum at the **La Brea Tar Pits** is a respected research and educational facility. If you're traveling with kids, they'll love the many hands-on exhibits. Beyond the museum's doors are the actual Tar Pits themselves, where you'll find yourself transported back more

than 40,000 years when saber-toothed cats called the Los Angeles basin home. The bubbly pits had entrapped more than 200 varieties of mammals, plants, birds, reptiles and insects from prehistoric times, and had been preserved as fossils. In 1914 the skeletal remains of a young Chumash Indian woman who lived 9,000 years ago was found in Pit 10. To this day approximately 8-12 gallons of black tar still bubble at the pits surface managing o entrap a collection of insects. There are replicas of life-sized mammals strategically placed about to remind us of what once roamed these lands years before. *Info:*

www.tarpits.org. Tel. 323/934-PAGE. Mid-Wilshire. 5801 Wilshire Boulevard. Open Monday-Friday 9am-5pm, weekends 10am-5pm. Admission is $7 adults, $4.50 children.

Working your way west along Wilshire Boulevard, you'll arrive at the **Los Angeles County Museum of Art** (LACMA). This county museum is now housed in two buildings, the original, now called LACMA East, and the newer LACMA West annex. You'll be able to explore more than 100,000 works of art: European masterpieces, cutting-edge contemporary art, works from America and Latin America, Islamic art, and one of the most comprehensive Korean art collections outside of Korea. LACMA is also known for hosting renowned exhibitions. *Info:* www.lacma.org. Tel. 323/857-6000. Mid-Wilshire. 5905 Wilshire Boulevard. Open every day except Wednesday from noon-8pm, 11am on weekends and open until 9pm on Friday. Admission is $9 adults, $5 children. The museum offers free admission after 5pm.

Across the street from LACMA West is the **Petersen Automotive Museum**. Spanning four floors, there are more 150 classic cars, trucks and motorcycles on display. You'll walk through—not past—exhibits and dioramas to experience the setting of early LA. There is also a display of celebrity-owned cars and vehicles made famous on both the small and big screens. *Info:* www.peterson.org. Tel. 323/930-CARS. Mid-Wilshire. 6060 Wilshire Boulevard. Open Tuesday-Sunday 10am-6pm. $10 adults, $5 children.

Hollywood

Tinseltown hasn't looked this good in decades. New restaurants, shops and entertainment venues continue to open, while landmarks, such as the **Hollywood Roosevelt Hotel**, have been returned to their glory days. Often described as Hollyweird, there still is an *anything goes* motto that works for this part of town. Even though most movies aren't filmed in Hollywood, there is still plenty of drama to observe. The sidewalks serve as the stage, the passersby as the cast and, with each passing day, the plot tends to thicken.

The heart of Hollywood is at the corner of **Hollywood and**

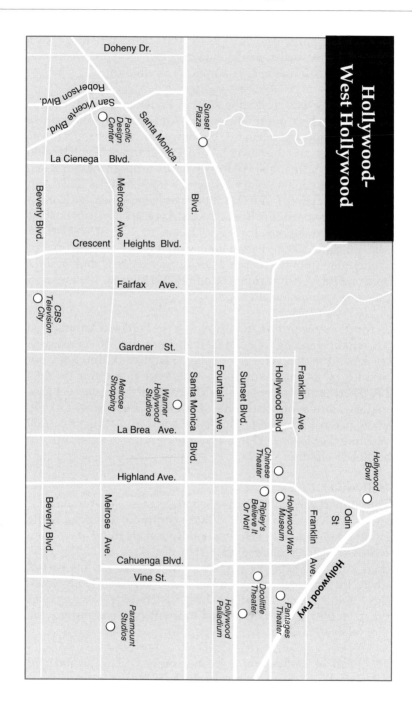

Highland (*see One Great Day in LA*) where the Hollywood and Highland shopping and entertainment complex is located, along with Grauman's Chinese Theater, the Kodak Theater, the Hollywood Roosevelt Hotel and the Hollywood Walk of Fame.

There are two notable theaters in this area, El Capitan and the Egyptian. **El Capitan,** built in 1926 and located next door to the building where they film  *Jimmy Kimmel Live*, is owned by the Walt Disney Company. The lavish interiors have been returned to their grandeur. Live stage shows often preempt movie screenings, which adds to the experience. Movie buffs will delight in knowing that Orson Welles premiered his classic 1939 film *Citizen Cane* here. *Info:* Tel. 323/461-8571. Hollywood. 6834 Hollywood Boulevard.

The 1922 **Egyptian Theatre** was also built by Sid Grauman of Grauman's Chinese Theatre fame. This was Hollywood's first movie palace and was the site of the very first movie premiere, *Robin Hood*, starring Douglas Fairbanks. Modeled after the Temple at Thebes, it is now home to **American Cinematheque**, a non-profit, viewer-supported cultural organization dedicated exclusively to the public presentation of the moving picture in all its forms. Screenings and special events are open to the public. Throughout the day *Forever Hollywood*, a documentary about the history of Hollywood, is shown with a prologue performed on the 1922 Wurlitzer organ. *Info:* www.egyptiantheatre.com. Tel. 323/461-9737. Hollywood. 6712 Hollywood Boulevard.

From Hollywood Boulevard, travel south on Highland Boulevard to Santa Monica Boulevard and head east. Right before you hit Van Ness Avenue, you'll see the **Hollywood Forever Cemetery** on your right. Established in 1899, this is the final resting place for many of those who shaped Hollywood. The most elaborate memorial is that of **Douglas Fairbanks**, featuring a reflecting pool fit for a king. Mel Blanc's marker poignantly reads *That's All Folks*. Fans of Tyrone Power can actually sit on his marker, which is a cement bench overlooking the pond. The mausoleum also contains many famous names, including Rudolph Valentino. Other noteworthy residents include Cecil B. DeMille, gangster Bugsy Siegel, Jayne Mansfield and Harry Cohn, just to name a very few. Keep in mind, this is a working cemetery and services are conducted daily. *Info:* www.hollywoodforever.com. Tel. 323/469-1181. Hollywood. 6000 Santa Monica Boulevard.

Just behind Hollywood Forever Cemetery is **Paramount Studios**, which is actually located at 5555 Melrose Avenue near Van Ness.

This is the only major classic studio still headquartered in Hollywood. After 9/11, all studios, except Universal Studios, which is also a theme park, cancelled their public tours. Now visitors, like yourself, are welcome to take part once again in a guided two-hour tour that gives a historical perspective and behind-the-scenes look at the day-to-day operations going on behind Paramount's iconic iron gates. Because filming is going on all around the lot, no no two tours are exactly the same. And, because this is a place of work and not a theme park, there is a chance you'll encounter a famous face. *Info:* www.paramount.com. Tel. 323/956-1777. Hollywood. 5555 Melrose Avenue. Tours are conducted Monday-Friday with advanced reservation. Admission is $35 per person and all participants must be 12 or older.

Two Frank Lloyd Wright houses are open to the public and a third, the Ennis-Brown House, Wright's last and largest concrete block house, is currently closed. The **Hollyhock House** at Barnsdall Art Park, which reopened in 2005 after five years of renovation, was completed in 1921 for oil heiress Aline Barnsdall and is Wright's second California structure. Rudolf Schindler, who assisted Wright on many projects, saw to the house's completion after Wright was fired from Barnsdall. *Info:* www.hollyhock.net. Tel. 323/644-6269. Hollywood. 4800 Hollywood Boulevard. Tours are Wednesday-Sunday from 12:30-3:30pm. Admission is $7 adults, $3 children.

Over on Glencoe Way in Hollywood is another one of Wright's homes that was built for two members of LA's avant-garde. **Samuel and Harriet Freeman** were introduced to Wright by none other than Aline Barnsdall. They asked Wright if he would design a home for them with a $10,000 budget (this was the early 1920s). He agreed, but the final textile block house, one of only three built in the Hollywood Hills, ended up costing more than twice that much. *Info:* Tel. 213/851-0671. 1962 Glencoe Way. Hollywood. Tours are conducted Saturdays only at 2pm and 4pm. Admission is $10; children under 6 are free.

The copper-vaulted dome that caps the whitewash stucco of **Griffith Observatory** can be

Other Backlot Tours

Except for Universal Studios, advanced reservations are required and the minimum age is 12. Hours and prices vary, so call ahead.

• **Universal Studios** in Universal City – part movie studio, part theme park, offering back lot tours, narrated tours from the comfort of a tram. Tel. 800/UNIVERSAL.

• **NBC Studios** in downtown Burbank – walking tour of the NBC broadcasting complex where you'll be able to view *The Tonight Show* set and other sets. *Info:* Tel. 818/840-3537.

• **Sony Pictures** in Culver City – you'll visit various sound stages, be privy to back lot anecdotes, and may even have a chance to visit the sets of *Jeopardy!* or *Wheel of Fortune. Info:* Tel. 323/520-8687.

• **Warner Brother Studios** in Burbank – visible from Universal's back lot, personalized VIP Electric Cart Tours include looks at live productions, recording stages and the prop shop. *Info:* Tel. 818/972-8687.

seen for miles. Built in 1935, this is where heaven meets earth on a daily basis. It used to be you could drive your car up to this landmark in the Hollywood Hills without a hitch. But after a five-year closure that resulted in a multi-million dollar renovation, the 72-year-old observatory, which reopened in November 2006 to great fanfare, now requires a bit more planning. The 199-space parking lot is temporarily closed, so you'll need to make advance reservations just to see the observatory and use shuttle buses based at the **Hollywood & Highland** shopping and entertainment center. The new and improved observatory features 60 astronomical exhibits that pertain to the tides, seasons, and phases of the moon. The new Gunther Depths of Space exhibit hall, built into the hillside, includes an enormous photomural that depicts a million galaxies not visible to the naked eye.

The observatory's dome houses the 300-seat planetarium (prior to the renovation there were 600 seats, but capacity was cut in half in order to provide a more satisfying experience for visitors). Although the observatory has always been a favorite movie backdrop, it was featured in the 1955 James Dean movie *Rebel Without A Cause* as well as the 1984 film *Terminator*, these days it's really gone Hollywood with the addition of a new Wolfgang Puck eatery on the premises. *Info:* www.griffithobservatory.org, Tel. 888/695-0888. Griffith Park. 2800 E. Observatory Road. Open Tuesday-Friday from 12pm-10pm, open 10am-10pm on weekends. Free admission, but shuttle reservations are required and are $8 adults, $4 children. Passengers can catch the shuttle near the LA Zoo or at Hollywood & Highland.

One of LA's most famous attractions is available to visitors 24-

hours a day, has no age restrictions, doesn't require an admission fee, and is the easiest to locate. All you have to do is cast your eyes towards the Hollywood Hills and you'll immediately see one of the city's oldest and most admired landmarks: the **Hollywood Sign**. It was unveiled in 1923 as an advertising gimmick to promote a gated housing tract called Hollywoodland. The original sign was replaced with a new one in 1979 at a cost of more than 12 times the original price. While climbing to the sign is prohibited, you will find one of the best photo opportunities for capturing the Hollywood sign down below in the flats at the corner of Sunset and Gower.

If you're visiting Los Angeles in the summer, be sure to take in a concert at either the **Hollywood Bowl** or the **Greek Theatre** *(see Best Activities chapter)*.

Beverly Hills/West Los Angeles
When locals refer to the *Westside*, as in "I live on the Westside," they want you to know that they reside in the better half of town. West Los Angeles includes Beverly Hills and West Hollywood, both separate cities from Los Angeles proper, as well as other upscale neighborhoods that are part of LA proper.

The image Beverly Hills has carved for itself is a land of expensive hotels, expensive shops and expensive homes. All true, but the city also has some lovely gardens that don't get half the attention that Rodeo Drive enjoys. So, I'll let you in on some of their best-kept secrets. The **Greystone Mansion and Park** is an 18.5-acre park located on the former Doheny estate. Edward Doheny was one of the first people to discover oil in Los Angeles, and his wealth allowed him to give a chunk of his ranch to his only son. Edward Jr. built a 55-room English Tudor mansion on the site in 1927, and today two areas of the former Doheny Mansion are open to the public: the formal garden with its large fountain, and the pool and inner courtyard. Many cultural events, which are open to the public, are held on the grounds throughout the year. *Info:* Tel. 310/550-4654. Beverly Hills. 905 Loma Vista Drive. Open daily 10am-5pm. Free admission.

Built in 1911 for the heiress of the Robinson Department Stores is the **Virginia Robinson Gardens**. When the childless Mrs. Robinson died in 1977, she left the estate to the County of Los Angeles. The interiors are just as they were when Mrs. Robinson died with all the original furnishings and artifacts neatly in place. You can stroll the six acres of gardens with more than 1,000 variety of plants. *Info:* www.robinson-gardens.com. Tel. 310/ 276-5367 ext. 100. Beverly Hills. Tours by appointment only Tuesday-Friday 10am or 1pm – 2 weeks notice required.

One of the most famous shopping streets in the world, right up there with Champs Elysee or the Via Veneto, is **Rodeo Drive**

(pronounced row-day-oh) located between Santa Monica and Wilshire Boulevards. Considered the crossroads of fashion and entertainment – I once saw Zsa Zsa Gabor strolling around in sweat pants and Richard Gere eating lunch at a sidewalk café – this street is famous for its designer boutiques and expensive merchandise. **Two Rodeo**, a quaint cobblestone destination, offers more shops and dining opportunities. You'll find even more shops along neighboring streets, such as Beverly Drive and Brighton Way. Department Store Row, along Wilshire Boulevard from Roxbury to Rodeo, is home to a handful of luxury retailers, including Neiman Marcus, Barneys New York and Saks Fifth Avenue, where Winona Ryder was arrested for shoplifting.

If you just spent a wad of money at Jimmy Choo on nearby Cañon Drive, you certainly don't want to take a chance on scuffing up your new shoes. So, instead, hop aboard the **Beverly Hills Trolley** for an exciting 40-minute trolley tour that will take you past many of the landmarks belonging to Beverly Hills, including Rodeo Drive and the esteemed neighborhoods lined with palm trees. *Info:* The narrated tour includes a bit of art and architectural history, and are offered on Saturdays only, on the hour, from 11am-4pm. The cost is $5 per person, $1 for children with free one-hour parking. Tel. 310/285-2438.

If you travel west along Wilshire Boulevard, you'll want to turn left onto Glendon Avenue near Westwood Village. At 1218 Glendon Avenue is **Westwood Memorial Park**, another final resting place for the famous. Marilyn Monroe was one of the first major stars to be interned her at the *Corridor of Memories*, and Playboy mogul Hugh Hefner purchased the crypt right next to Monroe's. Among those buried here are Natalie Wood, Frank Zappa, Robert Stack, Carroll O'Connor, Roy Orbison, Dean Martin, Peter Lawford, Truman Capote, and Rodney Dangerfield, to name a few. *Info:* Tel. 310/474-1579. Westwood. 1218 Glendon Avenue.

Now head to **Westwood Village** on the other side of Wilshire Boulevard. You can browse through shops, grab a bite to eat, or make a dash to through the village and to the other side where the entrance to UCLA is located. The renowned **Armand Hammer Museum of Art and Cultural Center** is located right on campus along with the **Franklin D. Murphy Sculpture Garden**, and the **Mildred E. Mathias Botanical Garden**. If you happen to be visiting Los Angeles during the last weekend of April, I highly recommend you plan a trip around the **Los Angeles Times Festival of Books**. Held outdoors on the UCLA campus and free to the public, this is one of the nation's largest literary events. There is also a wonderful area for children with storytelling and entertainment, plus booth after booth of nothing but books.

Malibu & The Beach Cities

For the most part, the beach cities are most appealing because of their leisurely activities: sunbathing, surfing, shopping, waterfront dining, and so on. Los Angeles County's beaches stretch from Malibu to the north all the way south to Long Beach covering some 70 miles of coastline.

Starting north in Malibu you'll stumble across the **Adamson House**, a 1930 Spanish Revival home located at **Malibu Lagoon State Beach**. A guided house tour will take you from room to room, where ceramic Malibu Tiles and fabulous craftsmanship have withstood the test of time. The gardens, which you can enjoy free of charge, thrive with blooming flora due to the beautiful beachfront setting. Adjoining the **Adamson House** is the **Malibu**

Lagoon Museum, where artifacts, rare photos and documents depicting Malibu's colorful history are found. The museum covers the early Chumash Indian era all the way up to the lavish lifestyles now found in the Malibu movie colony. *Info:* www.adamsonhouse.org. Tel. 310/456-8432. Malibu. 23200 Pacific Coast Highway. Open Wednesday-Saturday 11am-3pm.

 Admission is $5 adults, $3 children. Admission to the Malibu Lagoon Museum is free.

If you want to enjoy a picnic, grab some sandwiches from the deli at the **Ralph's** supermarket (23841 West Malibu Road – many celebrity residents shop here and the paparazzi know it) and have your lunch on the campus of **Pepperdine University** overlooking the Pacific Ocean. The views are unbelievable from up here. Try to plan your picnic on a weekend or during the summer when school is not in session. *Info:* 25255 Pacific Coast Highway.

Up in **Ramirez Canyon Park** is the former Malibu compound of **Barbra Streisand**, who donated the entire property, houses and all, to the state of California. She asked that her named be removed and entirely disassociated with the project a few years back when she didn't agree with the Coastal Commission's future plans. The compound is open to the public Wednesdays only by advanced reservation, and tours include the garden and her enclave of five homes. *Info:* Tel. 310/589-2850. Malibu. 5750 Ramirez Canyon Road.

Palos Verdes
Working your way south, Santa Monica is the next stop. In this chapter, pages 22-27, I've covered a number of great things to see and do in both Santa Monica and Venice. So keep heading south to the **Palos Verdes Peninsula**, where you'll travel along a breathtaking stretch known as Portuguese Bend. Along this scenic route is where **Wayfarer's Chapel** can be found. Known as the *glass church*, Lloyd Wright, who followed in his famous father's architectural footsteps, designed this transparent chapel using triangle shapes and huge, circular glass panes along with redwood and stone.

Free Polo Matches

For a truly unique experience, take in a free polo match at the **Will Rogers Polo Club** just off Sunset Boulevard in Pacific Palisades. Matches are held every weekend from April-October from 2-5pm on Saturdays and 10am-1pm on Sundays. You can bring a picnic lunch and make a day of it. *Info:* www.willrogerspolo.org. Tel. 310/454-8212. Will Rogers State Park in Pacific Palisades. 1501 Will Rogers State Park Road. Free.

You'll see why it's a popular site for weddings and for filming. *Info:* www.wayfarerschapel.org. Tel. 310/377-7919. Palos Verdes. 5755 Palos Verdes Drive South. Open daily 10am-5pm. Free.

San Pedro

Continue onward to San Pedro, part of LA proper and home to **Los Angeles Harbor**. At Berth 94 is the **S.S. Lane Victory Memorial Museum**, a 10,000-ton ship that served as an ammunition carrier during three wars: WWII, the Korean War, and the Vietnam War. While this museum remains static, during the summer months it does offer day cruises around the Los Angeles Harbor. *Info:* www.lanevictory.org. Tel. 310.519.9545. San Pedro. Berth 95 at Los Angeles Harbor. Open daily 9am-3pm. Admission is $3 adults, $1 children.

Up the hill at Angel's Gate Park is the **Korean Friendship Bell**, donated by the Republic of Korea to the residents of Los Angeles for the 1976 bi-centennial. The bell is fashioned after the 771 A.D. Bronze Bell of King Songdok, which is still on view in South Korea. The bell is rung from the outside with the strike of a wooden log and is heard just three times a year: Fourth of July, Korean Independence Day on August 15, and New Year's Eve. *Info:* At Gaffey and 37th Streets.

Visible from the nearby bluffs at Angel's Gate Park is the historic **Angel's Gate Lighthouse**, whose foghorn can be heard every 30 seconds. It has marked the entrance to the port since 1913, and sits perched on a 44-foot concrete square.

Long Beach

If you take the **Vincent Thomas Bridge**, which connects San Pedro to Long Beach, you'll see the historic 1936 **Queen Mary** as you near the city. Strolling the decks of this 1936 ocean liner is like going back in time. All the major celebrities from the '30s, '40s and '50s took their transatlantic voyages aboard the ship, and during World War II, when the Queen Mary was a troopship, Winston Churchill gave the orders for the D-Day Invasion. Since 1971, the ship has been a 365-stateroom hotel and attraction offering both self-guided and behind-the-scenes tours from stem to stern. *Info:* www.queenmary.com. Tel. 562/435-3511. Downtown Long

Beach. 1126 Queens Highway. Open daily 10am-6pm, until 9pm during the summer. Admission $27.95 adults, $16.95 children.

Moored next to the Queen Mary is the Cold War-era **Russian submarine** whose codename is **Scorpion**. You can tour both stealth and wealth in one visit. Combination tickets are available at the Queen Mary box office.

Across the harbor from the Queen Mary is the **Aquarium of the Pacific**, a 150,000 square-foot facility and the only aquarium dedicated to the riches of the Pacific Ocean. There are lots of interactive exhibits, both indoors and outside, and you can watch divers hand-feed the fish and mammals. Children really enjoy spending time here, putting their fingers in touch tanks, and taking part in various shows and demonstrations. *Info:* www.aquariumofpacific.org. Tel. 562/590-3100. Downtown Long Beach. 100 Aquarium Way. Open daily 9am-6pm. Admission is $19.95 adults, $11.95 children.

About a mile from the Aquarium of the Pacific is the **Museum of Latin American Art**, located in Long Beach's **East Village Arts District**. MoLAA, as its more commonly known, is the only museum in the west dedicated exclusively to promoting contemporary art hailing from Mexico, Central and South America, as well as the Spanish-speaking Caribbean. *Info:* www.molaa.com. Tel. 562/437-1689. Downtown Long Beach. 628 Alamitos Avenue. Open Tuesday-Friday 11:30am-7pm, Saturday 11am-7pm, Sunday 11am-6pm. Admission is $5 adults, $3 children.

Heading north through Long Beach to the Virginia Country Club neighborhood, you'll find **Rancho Los Cerritos**, an historic homestead that will transport you back to what life was like during the 1850s. It's one of the few remaining two-story adobes left in Southern California. Both this rancho and **Rancho Los**

Alamitos, located on the eastside of Long Beach, originate from Rancho Santa Gertrudes, the largest land grant ever bestowed in Southern California. Both ranchos offer living history tours, picnic areas and special events throughout the year. Rancho Los Alamitos features an historic ranch house and six barns situated on four acres of gardens. *Info:* Rancho Los Cerritos. www.rancholoscerritos.org. Tel. 562/570-1755. Northwest Long Beach. 4600 Virginia Road. Rancho Los Alamitos. www.rancholosalamitos.com. Tel. 562/431-3541. 6400 Bixby Hill Road. Both ranchos are open Wednesday-Sunday 1pm-5pm. Free – donations accepted.

If you want to a unique and romantic experience in Long Beach, try **Gondola Getaway** in east Long Beach along Alamitos Bay. Offered are one-hour rides in authentic Venetian gondolas. Sit back and enjoy the ride as a skilled gondolier ferries you through the picturesque canals of Naples Island, an exclusive Long Beach neighborhood fashioned after Venice, Italy. The ride includes a loaf of French bread, plus a plate of Italian meats and cheeses; you supply the wine or beverage of your choice. The best rides are those for just two, but there are some gondolas that can hold up to parties of 12. *Info:* www.gondolagetawayinc.com. Tel. 562/433-9595. Belmont Shore. 5437 Ocean Boulevard. $75 for two.

4. SAN DIEGO

Whether it's frolicking on the beach, strolling through downtown's Gaslamp Quarter, or enjoying a little animal magnetism at one of the county's zoos, San Diego is the ultimate Southern California getaway.

Downtown has morphed into a thriving urban center with many attractions void of walls and ceilings. Each borough, so to speak, offers its own brand of uniqueness. The **Gaslamp Quarter** is filled with fabulous restaurants, high-end hotels, and a great nightlife. **Little Italy** has more of a community feel, while the waterfront, near **Petco Park** where the San Diego Padres play their home games from April to October, feels open and spacious. A short distance away from downtown is **Balboa Park** and the world-famous **San Diego Zoo**. **Coronado Island**, home to the turreted and gabled Hotel Del Coronado, is its own hideaway just 10 minutes across the harbor. The beach communities are also just a flip-flop toss away and this is where you'll find **SeaWorld**, the vintage **Giant Dipper** roller coaster, **Mission Bay** and the pub haunts of **Pacific Beach**. Further up the coast are the resort communities of **La Jolla** and **Carlsbad** – home to **LegoLand** for those of you with kids.

ONE GREAT DAY IN SAN DIEGO

So little time, so much to do. And, the question that begs to be asked is *where the heck do you start?* You'll want to experience a bit of San Diego's great outdoors at **Torrey Pines State Reserve**, get a flavor of the city's history at **Old Town** and **Coronado Island**, and experience nightlife in the **Gaslamp Quarter**.

Begin with breakfast at **The Cottage** *(see San Diego Best Sleeps & Eats)* in the charming village of La Jolla. Housed in one of the city's original early 20th century cottages, breakfast is served daily until 11:30am. Get an early start and arrive when the restaurant opens at 7:30am. If it's a sunny morning, and it usually is, request an umbrella-shaded table on the restaurant's front porch.

Next, walk off that triple-egg omelet with a hike at **Torrey Pines State Reserve** near the Lodge at Torrey Pines. This 2,000-acre sprawl offers eight miles of trails, as well as guided nature walks on selected days. There are miles of unspoiled beaches, a lagoon, migrating birds, plenty of wildlife, and unusual insects and spiders. About the only thing you won't find here is a place to purchase food and drink, so come prepared with plenty of water and stay on marked trails only. *Info:* www.torreypine.org. Tel.

858/755-2063. From Interstate 5, exit Carmel Valley Road and head west for about 1.5 miles until you reach Coast Highway. Turn left and proceed along the beach for approximately one mile. The park entrance is on the right just before the steep upgrade. Parking fees are $6.

After leaving Torrey Pines State Reserve, get back on Interstate 5 heading south to **Old Town San Diego State Historical Park**.

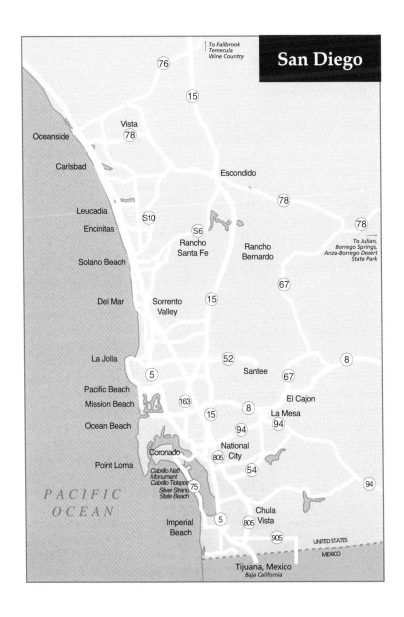

ALTERNATIVE PLAN
When you've got just hours to explore San Diego, passage aboard the **Old Town Trolley Tour** is time and money well spent. Tickets are less than $30 per person ($13 for kids). There are eight key stops, including Old Town State Park, Cruise Ship Terminal, Seaport Village, Horton Plaza, Coronado Island, Balboa Park and the Convention Center/Waterfront. You can get on and off as you please, and once you've made a complete loop the ride is over. Tour guides provide interesting anecdotes, humorous stories, and a detailed history of the city. *Info*: www.trustedtours.com. Tel. 800/213-2474.

Not only is this historic enclave the birthplace of San Diego, it is also the beginning of California's history. In 1769, Father **Junipero Serra** established the first of the 21 California missions on Presidio Hill in Old Town, and the ruins of that mission can still be seen at **Presidio Park**. Much of the state's early life of Mexican and American pioneers is recaptured daily. There is a collection of restored buildings with others reconstructed to look like the original on the same foundations. La Casa de Estudillo was built in 1827 by the commander of the presidio and was one of the town's first adobe houses. Other interesting stops include a single-story façade housing a replica of the city's first drugstore with displays of pharmaceutical memorabilia and artifacts. Guided tours of Old Town are conducted daily. **Bazaar del Mundo** is the only commercial element of Old Town. It features a collection of shops and restaurants with strolling mariachis and folkloric dancers. Many of

Bazaar del Mundo's buildings are also historic or have been replicated to look like adobes, and the entire marketplace is centered around a lovely courtyard. *Info:* www.oldtownsandiego.org. Tel. 619/291-4903. San Diego. Off Interstate 5 at the Old Town Avenue exit.

Next stop: **Coronado Island**. You'll continue south on Interstate 5 and follow the signs to the Coronado Bay Bridge, which leads to the "island" which is actually a peninsula. Begin your tour at the **Hotel Del Coronado History Gallery**. Much of Coronado's history resides under the turrets of "The Del." Even if you are not

a registered hotel guest, a free self-guided tour detailing more than a century of history is on display. Vintage photos of kings and queens, American presidents, foreign dignitaries and Hollywood idols offer a glimpse into the past. Displays of guest records and other hotel artifacts demonstrate how fashion, technology and leisure travel have evolved during the past century. One-hour guided tours, offered at a nominal fee, are available. Don't rush off as there is plenty to admire at the Hotel Del, from the Victorian lobby and the original birdcage elevator to the gorgeous grounds and ocean views. *Info:* www.hoteldel.com. Tel. 619/435-6611. Coronado. 1500 Orange Avenue.

After leaving the Hotel Del, stroll along **Orange Avenue** where there are many shops and restaurants on either side of the street. You may want to take a look at the gabled **Meade House**, located at 1101 Star Park Circle not far from town. Built in 1896, it served as the winter home of author **L. Frank Baum** who penned the classic tale of *The Wizard of Oz*. Baum wrote four of his books while living on Coronado Island, and he designed the signature crown chandeliers for the resort.

Now it's on to **Mission Beach**. Your one and only stop here is at the **Giant Dipper Roller Coaster** at Belmont Park, one of only two wooden seaside roller coasters remaining in California (the other is in Santa Cruz). It's a rickety ride at a brisk speed, and from the top you get a great view of the ocean. Believe it or not, couples have chosen the roller coaster—in motion—as the backdrop for their wedding. Belmont Park also has a lot of other amusements geared for every member of the family, as well as restaurants. *Info:* www.belmontpark.com. Tel. 619/488-1548. Mission Beach. 3190 Mission Boulevard. Free admission to park; rides priced individually. Open daily from 11am.

Get Yer Adrenalin Rush!

San Diego Wild Animal Park's Roar & Snore – from April through October spend the night in a tent along one of the rugged trails with elephants, rhinos and tigers roaming just feet away. **Biplane and Air Combat Adventures** – Don a helmet and a pair of goggles and enjoy the ride of your life aboard a vintage 1929 open cockpit biplane. Tel. 760/438-7680. **Palomar Plunge** – Starting at the Palomar Observatory, experienced cyclists can descend 5,000 feet at breakneck speed along a 13-mile road.

From Mission Beach, head to **downtown San Diego** and the bustling **Gaslamp Quarter**. Begin the evening with a sunset cocktail atop the Manchester Grand Hyatt on the harbor *(see San Diego Best Sleeps & Eats)* where you'll encounter fabulous views from several stories up. From here you can walk to the Gaslamp Quarter for dinner at **Bella Luna** *(see San Diego Best Sleeps & Eats)* on Fifth Street, featuring fabulous Italian fare and a romantic setting. After dinner, head to one of the clubs to enjoy some live music. Down the street is **Croce's**, owned by the late singer-songwriter Jim Croce's wife, which features live jazz and R&B. **Café Sevilla** on nearby Fourth Street is known for its live flamenco shows.

If just the thought of riding a roller coaster has you feeling queasy, then you may want to skip Mission Beach altogether and head straight to downtown San Diego to the **San Diego Aircraft Carrier Museum** where the USS Midway, the longest-serving aircraft carrier in U.S. Navy history, is anchored at Navy Pier. Take a self-guided "boiler to bridge" audio tour featuring more than 40 exhibits. *Info*: www.midway.org. Tel. 619/544-9600. Downtown. 910 N. Harbor Drive.

Best Mexican Eats

Some of the best **Mexican food** can be found at a host of brightly painted roadside dives whose names, for whatever reason, all end in "berto's." There is **Roberto's, Alberto's, Rigoberto's** and so on. These stands serve fresh, authentic, border-style Mexican food: carne asada burritos, shredded beef tacos, and the classic fish tacos, at very cheap prices. You'll find them in Pacific Beach, Mission Beach, Hillcrest, and elsewhere.

A FANTASTIC SAN DIEGO WEEKEND

With an entire weekend ahead of you you'll have an opportunity to spend more time by the beach, visiting some of the landmarks, such as **Balboa Park** or **Cabrillo National Park**, and paying a lengthy visit to one of the animal or theme parks. Food choices run the gamut from fresh seafood and fine wine to giant burritos purchased from local taco stands.

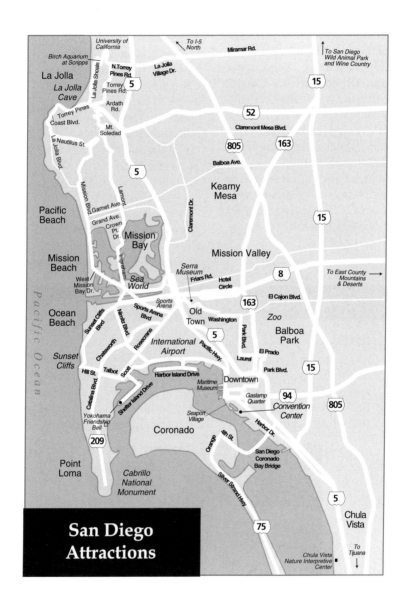

San Diego Attractions

Friday evening
Check into **Crystal Pier Hotel and Cottages** (*see San Diego's Best Sleeps & Eats*), located on the pier in Pacific Beach. Enjoy the sunset, uncork a bottle of wine, and take a stroll along the boardwalk toward Mission Beach and **Belmont Park**. Take a ride on the historic 1925 **Giant Dipper Roller Coaster**, go head-to-head on the bumper cars, or take a twirl on the carousel.

Travel Note: The Crystal Pier Hotel and Cottages can be an extremely romantic getaway. If you're traveling with kids, you may want to stay at a larger, more full-service hotel. **Paradise Point** (*see San Diego Best Sleeps & Eats*), located on Mission Bay just down the road, is better suited to couples traveling with children.

Saturday
Wake up to breakfast at **The Broken Yolk** (Tel. 858/270-9655, 1815 Garnet), a Pacific Beach staple for years with a never-ending line to prove its popularity. The rooftop patio has the best tables. After breakfast, head to **Cabrillo National Monument**, which commemorates explorer Juan Rodriguez Cabrillo's inaugural landing at San Diego Bay on September 28, 1542, marking the first time Europeans had set foot on what was to become the western part of the United States. Check out the small museum, as well as the excellent views of **San Diego Harbor**. The **Point Loma Lighthouse**, also located here, has been returned to its 1880s splendor and ranger-led talks and tours are open to the public. *Info:* Tel. 619/557-5450. Point Loma. 1800 Cabrillo Memorial Drive.

Next head to **Balboa Park**, the pride of San Diego and a real showpiece among city parks. Larger than New York's Central Park and older than San Francisco's Golden Gate Park, this oasis of culture contains more than two dozen museums all within close proximity to one another. You'll have time to visit just one or two venues at the most. You'll definitely want to visit the **San Diego Musuem of Art**, with its collection of European works from the Italian Renaissance and Spanish Baroque periods, as well as masterpieces from Asia and the United States. The **Ruben E. Fleet Science Museum** is ideal for kids. There are more than eight distinct gardens in the park, including the **Japanese Friendship Garden**, which originated as a teahouse during the 1915-16 Panama-California Exposition. The gardens now lie on two acres near the Spreckels Organ Pavilion. Start out on one of the garden's meandering paths, which will eventually lead to various outposts, including the Zen garden, koi pond and bonsai exhibit. If time allows, sign-up for one of the weekend classes, from sushi making to the art of calligraphy. *Info:* www.balboapark.org. Tel. 619/239-0512. The Botanical Building, outdoor gardens, and some selected attractions are free of charge; most museums charge a nominal fee.

ALTERNATIVE PLAN
Not into museums and gardens? Then go to the world-famous **San Diego Zoo**, also in Balboa Park. Plan to spend the entire day among the menagerie of 4,000 inhabitants of rare and endangered animals. Animal shows are scheduled just about every hour, and strolling characters provide photo ops. Guided bus tours are offered, but it's more fun to go on your own. *Info:* www.sandiegozoo.org. Tel. 619/231-1515. Balboa Park. Park Boulevard & Zoo Place. Open daily 9am-4pm, until 9pm during the summer. Admission: $33 adults, $22 ages 3-11.

You're likely a little tired after walking around Balboa Park, so head to the harbor and enjoy a relaxing cruise around the **San Diego Harbor**. There are two companies that offer narrated, one-hour tours of either the north or south end of the bay (**San Diego Harbor Excursion**, www.sdhe.com, and **Hornblower Cruises**, www.hornblower.com). Highlights, depending on which tour you take, include the Coronado Bridge, naval aircraft carriers and other military ships, the submarine base, Point Loma (where your day began) and both Shelter and Harbor Islands. After you disembark, walk along the water-

front and admire the fleet of historic and notable ships afloat at the **Maritime Museum of San Diego.**

In keeping with the seafaring theme, grab dinner at one of San Diego's seafood restaurants along the harbor. I recommend the **Fish Market** along Harbor Avenue for a casual meal or **Top of the Market**, located above the Fish Market, for a more upscale dining experience. Take your pick and, if you are not a seafood fan, then head to nearby **Kansas City BBQ** (*see San Diego Best Sleeps & Eats*) along Market Street across from Seaport Village. Afterwards, if you still have some energy left, head to the **Gaslamp Quarter**, specifically Fifth Avenue, and check out some of the bars and lounges for live entertainment.

Sunday

Today is a good day to visit some of San Diego's unique neighborhoods. Begin with an inexpensive, but filling breakfast at **Sun Café** on Market Street near the Gaslamp Quarter. Housed in one of the oldest buildings in the area, this cash-only diner was featured in the film *Almost Famous*.

From almost famous to truly infamous, it's on to **Little Italy** just north of the Gaslamp Quarter. This community, as richly ethnic as New York's Mulberry Street, began growing roots in the 1920s when the bulk of the city's Italian citizens settled here during the height of the tuna fishing fleet. Begin your Little Italy sojourn along **India Avenue**, visiting the shops, markets and eateries that  make this enclave unique. If you're a preservationist, **Architectural Salvage** carries relics pulled from vintage homes, such as windows, doors, heater grates, crystal doorknobs and other retro gems.

Up the block is **Disegno Italiano**, which stocks streamline Italian kitchen appliances and furnishings. Stop for lunch at **Filippi's,** where red-checked cloths cloak modest tables and Chianti bottles dangle from above. The restaurant also features a fabulous deli and market. Just off India Street are the **Fir Street Cottages**, a tidy row of brightly painted homes that have been converted into a jungle of unique shops. Info: www.littleitalysd.com.

Say ciao to Little Italy and move on to the fabulous and funky streets of **Hillcrest** located uptown near Balboa Park. Quirky and fun loving, this vibrant neighborhood is home to San Diego's gay community. Gay or straight, it's a great place to spend a few hours roaming through the bustling streets, prowling the stylish thrift stores, and admiring the Craftsman-style bungalows. **University Avenue** and **Washington Street** are considered the major east-west thoroughfares, while Fourth, Fifth and Sixth Avenues connect Hillcrest to downtown San Diego. Since it's Sunday, make a quick stop to the **Hillcrest Farmers Market** to browse the fruit stands, admire the crafts for sale, and do some people watching. You'll find a bulk of unique shops along University and Fifth Avenues, such as **Taste Artisan Cheese & Gourmet, Wine Steals** wine bar, and **Blue Stocking Books**, the last of the independent booksellers. *Info:* www.hillquest.com.

After a dizzying day in Hillcrest, jump on Interstate 5 and head south to the Coronado Bridge for a farewell dinner at the waterfront **1500 Ocean** at the Hotel Del Coronado. If you're more inclined to have just drinks and light fare, then grab a table at the resort's clubby **Babcock & Story**, an upscale oceanfront pub. After dinner, if there's time and you feel up to it, stroll down **Orange Avenue** to admire the shops and boutiques.

If you had your heart set on visiting one or more of San Diego's **theme parks**, you'll need to rearrange this plan and set aside one day for each. **SeaWorld**, located on Mission Bay, is a 150-acre marine life park and home to the killer whale Shamu. *Info:* www.4adventure.com. Tel. 619/226-3901. Mission Bay. 500 Sea World Drive. Open year round with seasonal hours. Admission: $56 adults, $46 ages 3-9. **San Diego Wild Animal Park**, located in Escondido, allows visitors to get up-close and personal with the likes of zebras, giraffes, and lions. *Info:* www.sandiegozoo.org. Tel. 760/747-8702. Escondido. 15500 San Pasqual Valley Road.

Open daily from 9am-4pm, until 8pm during the summer. Admission: $28.50 adults, $17.50 ages 3-11. **LEGOLAND**, located in Carlsbad, features 50 rides and attractions geared towards kids ages 12 and under. *Info:*  www.legoland.com. Tel. 858/ 918-5346. Carlsbad. One Lego Drive. Open daily from 10am-5pm, until 8pm during the summer. Admission: $57 adults, $47 ages 3-12.

A WONDERFUL WEEK IN SAN DIEGO

With a week in San Diego, you've got time to get a real flavor for the city and its history. You'll see the best of the best in the **northern part** of San Diego County, as well as downtown San Diego and its environs, such as **Old Town**, **Balboa Park**, **Coronado Island** and, of course, the **beaches**. You'll visit the best museums, spend a day at the theme park of your choice, and get close to nature on the bottom of the desert floor.

RECOMMENDED PLAN: Spend two nights in **North County San Diego** with one day at **Legoland** and the other at **San Diego Wild Animal Park**. Then head south for the remainder of your trip, with a day to explore in and around **downtown San Diego**, another day to visit **Balboa Park**, one day to spend at the beach, and another to take a day trip to either the historic silver mining town of **Julian**, the arid **Anza-Borrego Desert**, or **Tijuana, Mexico**.

Downtown San Diego

A visit to downtown is more of a sensory experience than that of a sightseeing mission. There are no major attractions to speak of,

Don't Miss ...

- **Balboa Park** – two-dozen museums, the world-famous San Diego Zoo and the Old Globe Theatre
- **Hotel Del Coronado** – a beautiful historic landmark
- **Gaslamp Quarter** – the pulse of San Diego's social life; scores of shops, restaurants and clubs housed in the original brick and mortar buildings
- **Giant Dipper Roller Coaster** – 1925 wooden roller coaster in Mission Beach

but there is still plenty to experience nonetheless. **Downtown San Diego** has the feel of both a modern metropolis and a small town with skyscrapers existing next to turn-of-the-century relics. Within a single square-mile grid are vibrant neighborhoods, fabulous shopping, galleries and a breathtaking waterfront.

Begin at the **Civic Center** and head down **Broadway** to the historic **U.S. Grant Hotel**, built in 1910 and recently reopened after a two-year renovation. Ulysses S. Grant Jr. wanted to honor his father, the 18th President of the United States, so he presented him with a monumental gift: a grand hotel bearing his name. The hotel's bars and restaurants are open to the public, so stop in if only to look around the lobby where a lovely tea is served every afternoon.

Across the street from the U.S. Grant Hotel, behind the NBC Studios, is **Horton Plaza**, with its eccentric architecture, kaleidoscopic colors and multi-levels of outdoor shopping and entertainment opportunities including Nordstrom, Macy's and hundreds of specialty shops. To the east of this mega mall, stretching south to the waterfront, is the historic **Gaslamp Quarter**, where

a rash of Victorian structures have been restored to their brick and mortar splendor. As I've mentioned before in this chapter, this is the pulse of San Diego's social scene where the city's best restaurants, bars and nightclubs are lined up like dominos.

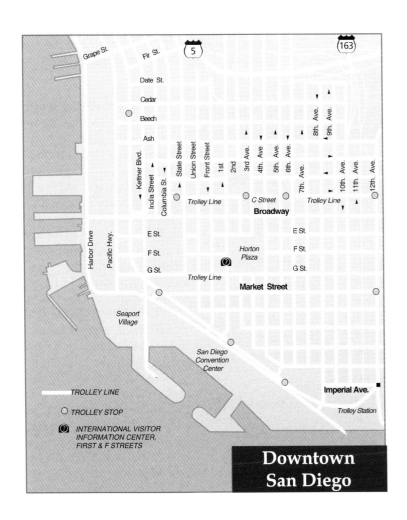

Downtown San Diego

To the east of the Gaslamp Quarter is the aptly named **East Village**, which is a neighborhood in transition and, because of its close proximity to the Gaslamp Quarter, may even be considered an extension of it as well. This area south of Market still has a very industrial feel, but has seen its stock rise with the 2004 opening of **Petco Park**. You can watch the **San Diego Padres** play on their home turf from April to October. Definitely check out the stadium, whether it's baseball season or not. Off-season tours are offered to the public.

Balboa's Free Entry Days

On any given Tuesday you can enjoy **free admission** to select **Balboa Park museums**:
First Tuesday:
Reuben H. Fleet Science Center
Second Tuesday:
Museum of Photographic Arts
San Diego Historical Society Museum and Research Archives
Third Tuesday:
Japanese Friendship Gardens
San Diego Museum of Art
San Diego Museum of Man
Mingei International Museum
San Diego Art Institute
Fourth Tuesday:
San Diego Automotive Museum
Hall of Nations free film
San Diego Hall of Champions Sports Museum

Go back to Fifth Street, which dead-ends into waterfront where the **Harbor** and **Embarcadero Districts** comprise downtown's western and southern boundaries. If you enjoy maritime history, then you'll want to spend some time at the **Maritime Museum of San Diego**, where a fleet of historic vessels and the flagship **Star of India** are moored. Nearby is the Cruise Ship Terminal, as well as local charter boat companies that ferry passengers about the harbor for dinner cruises and seasonal whale watching adventures, which are offered December through April. As the road bows eastward, you'll catch your first glimpse of the **Midway Aircraft Carrier Museum** at Navy Pier. The *U.S.S. Midway* enjoyed a fascinating 47-year military career from WWII to Desert Storm in the early 1990s. Onboard, from the hangar deck to the flight deck, are more than 35 exhibits.

Seaport Village, which fronts The Embarcadero, is an outdoor shopping and entertainment complex. Nearby is a collection of lovely public parks where you can witness sailboats passing under the Coronado Bridge. Downtown's outlying areas, such as **Little Italy** and **Hillcrest**, have also enjoyed a renaissance during the last decade.

Just north of downtown is the 1200-acre **Balboa Park**, boasting a couple of dozen museum, indoor and outdoor theaters, public sports complex, and the world-famous San Diego Zoo. You could easily spend the day either at the zoo *or* scouring the park's museums, but not both as there just simply isn't enough time in the day. Built for the 1915-16 Panamerican Exposition, the Moorish-style buildings were intended as temporary housing for the fair's exhibits. Nearly 100 years later the elegant facades, foyers and fountains house permanent museums and attractions.

Make a point to visit the **San Diego Museum of Art**, which exhibits an impressive collection of fine art including paintings from the Renaissance period. Also topping my list is the **Museum of Man**, which blends permanent exhibits on local indigenous populations with such diverse visiting themes as Egyptian mummies. Balboa Park is also home to the **Old Globe Theater**, where the works of Shakespeare are presented on stage in a building replicated to look like the original 16th century variety in London.

One of my favorite exhibits, the **International Cottages**, is only open on Sunday. This cluster of two dozen homes represents countries from around the world. Also within Balboa Park is the **Marston House**, a stately Arts and Crafts-style mansion built in 1905 for prominent San Diegan George Marston. Furnished in period-style décor, the house is listed on the National Register of Historic Places and open to the public for tours.

Tijuana, Mexico

San Diego is often heralded as being the **Two Nation Vacation** because of its close proximity to the Mexican border – just 16 miles from downtown. Visitors to Southern California always seem a bit surprised at just how easy it is to cross the border, even in our post 9/11 world. It may seem obvious, but a word of caution is in order: although Mexico is just a short distance away, you are still venturing into a foreign country. It's wise to obey and respect the laws of the land to ensure your own personal safety.

I strongly recommend that you **don't drive into Mexico**, and if you're renting a car most agencies prohibit you from taking their vehicles across the border. Instead, you can take the convenient **San Diego Trolley**, also known as the Tijuana Trolley because of its destination to the Mexican border. At the final stop on the U.S. side, disembark and walk across to the border and into Mexico. Or drive south on Interstate 5 to the U.S. border town of San Ysidro; park at facilities near the border and walk across. Once on the other side, you can either walk to the main thrust of Tijuana or hail a cab. If you do decide to drive, you should purchase Mexican auto insurance either prior to reaching the border or at the border crossing.

Once your reach **Tijuana**, or TJ as it's commonly referred to, you'll want to head to the shopping and entertainment district along **Avenida Revolucion**. Here you can shop for handcrafted furnishings, lace, silver, jewelry, and lots of other merchandise. It's all reasonably priced, but it is also common practice to haggle. Tijuana is a duty-free zone where US currency, pesos, traveler's checks and major credit cards are accepted; however, street vendors will only accept cash in U.S. dollars or pesos.

After shopping, head to the **Caliente-Jai-Alai Fronton Palacio,** the oldest building in Tijuana, where fans of jai alai find it hard to keep their eye on the ball when it's traveling at speeds of more than 160 miles per hour. If you have time, the nearby **Caliente Race Track** hosts greyhound races. You can also take in a **bullfight** at El Toreo.

San Diego's North County

Never will you experience a more diverse region than in San Diego's North County. Within 90 minutes you can go from the sandy coast to the arid desert, passing picturesque lakes and remote villages along the way. Aside from the beach communities, for which San Diego is most famous, most of North County remains undiscovered by tourists. Unlike its southern counterpart, known for its many attractions and urban sophistication, North County San Diego is brimming with award-winning golf courses, renowned resorts, rugged terrain and, would you believe, good ol' apple pie.

The coastal communities include **San Onofre, Oceanside, Carlsbad, Leucadia, Solana Beach, Del Mar**, and **La Jolla** (La Jolla is a close call as it straddles the line). Here you'll discover some of the area's best beaches and surf spots, as well as a few of San Diego's key attractions.

Great Surfing Beaches

- **San Onofre State Beach -** located off Interstate 5 at Basilone Road in San Onofre
- **Swami's Beach -** located along Highway 101 just south of Encintas Boulevard in Encintas
- **Black's Beach** – at Torrey Pines State Reserve in La Jolla

La Jolla & Del Mar

La Jolla, the furthest point south, is where you'll find the **Birch Aquarium at Scripps**. Touted as the largest oceanographic museum in the nation, you'll discover the marine sciences through interactive exhibits. Be sure to bring the kids to the rocky tide pools overlooking the coastline, where underwater habitats and marine plant life can be observed. *Info:* www.aquarium.ucsd.edu. Tel. 858/534-FISH. La Jolla. 2300 Expedition Way. Open daily 9am-5pm. Admission: $10 adults, $9 seniors, $7.50 youth.

If you prefer art to aquariums, then head to La Jolla's **Museum of Contemporary Art** overlooking the ocean. The MCA's focus is on the visual arts with a vast permanent collection of works on display, as well as traveling exhibits. *Info:* www.mcasd.org. Tel. 858/454-3541. La Jolla. 700 Prospect Street. Open daily from 11am to 5pm, until 7pm on Thursday; closed Wednesday. Admission: General admission $10, $5 seniors and military with ID, 25 years and younger are free.

For two weeks starting in mid-June at the Del Mar Race Track, the annual **Del Mar County Fair** makes its way to town with livestock competitions, traditional carnie rides and games. Headliner bands and evening fireworks create large crowds after dark. Then from late July through early September, horseracing season gets underway Wednesday-Monday. *Info:* www.dmtc.com. Tel. 858/755-1141. Del Mar. 2260 Jimmy Durante Boulevard.

Every Sunday, from June through September, the public is invited to the **San Diego Polo Club** in neighboring **Rancho Santa Fe** to watch the polo matches at 1:30pm and 3pm. Tickets are just $5 per person. *Info:* www.sandiegopolo.com. Tel. 858/481-9217. Rancho Santa Fe. 14555 El Camino Real.

Oceanside

Continue north on Interstate 5 until you reach Oceanside. The town, home to the Marine Corp.'s **Camp Pendleton**, has a very strong military presence. California's 18th mission, the **Mission San Luis Rey**, is also located in Oceanside. This is the largest of the 21 missions in the state and, as such, is dubbed the King of the

Missions. Established on June 13, 1798, it was named for St. Louis IX, King of France, patron of the Secular Franciscan Order.

The museum houses exhibits relating to the colorful history of San Luis Rey with a collection of artifacts from various periods. Of special interest are such sacred treasures as the classical and baroque designs of the church altar; the original baptismal font, made of hand-hammered copper by the Indians; the Moorish design of the pulpit ; and the 1770 statue of the Immaculate Conception. Take some time to visit the 1798 cemetery, the oldest burial ground in North San Diego County, which contains early grave markers, mausoleums, and an 1830 monument erected in honor of the Luiseno Indians who contributed greatly to the construction of the mission. If you are here at the beginning of the summer, make a point to attend the popular **Fiesta** commemorating the mission's founding with rides and entertainment. *Info:* www.sanluisrey.org. Tel. 760/757-3651. Oceanside. 4050 Mission Avenue. Open daily 10am-4pm. Admission: $5 adults, $3 ages 18 and under.

Head down towards the beach to stroll along the **Oceanside Pier**, California's longest pier stretching nearly 2,000 feet from the shore. The original pier was constructed in 1888 with the present concrete structure taking its place in 1925 with wooden portions added in the late 1980s. On a clear day you can see La Jolla and Catalina Island from the pier's end. *Info:* Located at the end of Pier View Way in downtown Oceanside.

Julian
From Oceanside, motor inland towards Escondido and onward through the back roads of San Diego County. You'll wind your way through the town of Ramona, and eventually you'll come to **Dudley's Bakery** in Santa Ysabel at the crossroads of Highways 78 and 79. This modest bakery is famous for its fresh-baked raisin

bread, so grab a loaf to enjoy later back at your hotel. Make a quick stop along Highway 79 to the **Santa Ysabel Indian Mission**, an extension of the San Diego Mission de Alcala and the site of an Indian burial ground. Admission is free, but donations are accepted.

From here, it's just a short drive to **Julian**. This unique town, with its four mild seasons (yes, it gets a light dusting of snow most winters) is so unlike anything typical of Southern California. The country road that leads from Interstate 5 to this former mining town is as enjoyable as the destination itself. Aside from **eating apple pie**, browsing through a few shops, and paying a visit to a couple of the town's wineries, there isn't a whole lot to do, but the false-front stores, wooden sidewalks and historic buildings make for a unique afternoon. My family and I make the pilgrimage every fall for the annual apple harvest, and Julian is one of those destinations I like to recommend to visitors.

Once you arrive in Julian, park the car and head to **Main Street** where the hub of shops and cafes are located. Stop by the 120-year-old **Julian Drug Store** at 2134 Main Street. The soda fountain and its marble counter haven't changed since it was first installed in 1932. Next, stroll down to the **Julian Cider Mill** at 2103 Main Street where apples are pressed for cider. You can also watch apples being dipped into vats of caramel, as well as honeybees producing golden syrup from their beehive. **Country Carriages**, Tel. 760/765-1471, offers afternoon and early evening rides in horse-drawn carriage. You can usually find the horse and carriage stationed outside the Julian Drug Store in between rides. The **Eagle & High Peak Mines**, Tel. 760/765-0036, offers guided tours into a 1,000-foot hard-rock tunnel where you'll actually see the gold mining and milling processes used more than a century ago. Call ahead to book your tour.

Mom's Pies at 2119 Main Street tempts passersby by placing

 workers in front of the large picture window to assemble their pies. The line is long at Mom's, but my favorite place for a slice is at **The Julian Pie Company** at 2225 Main Street, which offers

outdoor seating on both its front porch and back patio. There are also two wineries near town, both located on Julian Orchards Road, with tasting rooms. **J. Jenkins Winery** is at 1255 Julian Orchards Road and the **Menghini Winery** is at 1150 Julian Orchards Road.

Travel Note: If you're leaving from downtown San Diego, you can hop on Route 8 to Route 79 or Route 15 and pick up Route 78 in Escondido.

Anza-Borrego Desert State Park

In just 45 minutes you can travel from the alpine setting of Julian to the barren **Anza-Borrego Desert State Park** along Highway 78. If you can plan it so that you arrive at Julian in the morning, then you'll have time to spend the afternoon on the bottom of the desert floor. It's an amazing change of scenery as you make your descent towards the Anza-Borrego Desert State Park, which is so unlike the rest of San Diego that most visitors are amazed at the contrasting landscapes presented to them in such a relatively short distance.

Traveling from downtown San Diego — or any other part of the county for that matter — you quickly realize how vastly the scenery can change. The park, about a two-hour drive, was established in 1933 in part to preserve the habitat of the bighorn sheep and, although this majestic animal is slowly headed for extinction due to illness and changes in their habitat, you are still likely to see the herds roaming the open terrain.

You'll want to give yourself plenty of time to reach the park, which covers more than 600,000 acres of nature trails, scenic views and unusual topography. **Borrego Springs**, a rustic resort community within the park, offers some recreation options as well as a handful of lodging choices. As soon as you reach the park, your first stop should be the expansive **Visitors Center** at the west end of Palm Canyon Drive. Inside the center you'll discover exhibits, maps, books and a knowledgeable staff that can provide you with valuable tips on the area. There is also a 15-minute slide presentation that will further acquaint you with this desert region. There are magnificent hiking trails for all abilities, and the country's largest natural palm oasis is located within the park. You can tour the desert floor on your own, on horseback, or on a guided off-road vehicle tour.

If you want to take your time enjoying both Julian and the Anza-Borrego State Desert Park without feeling rushed, consider taking an overnight jaunt inland. See the listing for Julian/Anza-Borrega in my *Best Sleeps & Eats* chapter.

5. ORANGE COUNTY

Orange County, which has been overshadowed by Los Angeles for much of its existence, is finally getting the attention it deserves. For years the only thing behind the "Orange Curtain," a term referring to the county's conservative stance, was Disneyland and little else. Then poof! Suddenly everyone was talking about *The OC*, both the television series and the county. Next came a dose of reality in the form of MTV's *Laguna Beach: The Real OC* and, more recently, the Bravo series *Real Housewives of Orange County*. None of these shows really paint an accurate portrait of Orange County, but they're amusing nonetheless.

Spend most of your time in the coastal cities where you'll discover the most magnificent waterfront resorts. Orange County also has some great shopping destinations, as well as unique cultural and historic stops, such as the **Mission San Juan Capistrano**. Of course, you may have plans to spend a day at **Disneyland Resort**, home to the original Disneyland theme park and the newer **Disney's California Adventure**. **Knott's Berry Farm**, located in Buena Park, is another theme park option with more hair-raising rides. If you enjoy a mix of politics and history, you'll want to head to the northern part of the county for a visit to the **Richard Nixon Library and Birthplace** in Yorba Linda.

ONE GREAT DAY IN ORANGE COUNTY

You'll certainly want to make the most of your time, and the best place to do so is along the coast. Start with a nature walk in **Huntington Beach**, then you'll travel south along Pacific Coast Highway visiting the coastal communities of **Newport Beach** and **Laguna Beach**.

Wake up, it's going to be a beautiful day. Don't be disappointed if you draw back the curtains at your luxe seaside resort only to find a thick marine layer suspended like heavy drapery over the surf. This is a typical morning along the coast, and the fog will most likely lift by noon. Start your day with a leisurely hike at the **Bolsa Chica Ecological Reserve** in Huntington Beach. Comprised of 330 acres and home to nearly 200 species of birds, this coastal wetlands is truly a force of nature. Afterwards, drive south on Pacific Coast Highway to downtown Huntington Beach, and enjoy breakfast at the end of the pier at **Ruby's Diner**. The menu offers your basic breakfast coupled with the most incredible ocean views.

After you leave Huntington Beach, continue south towards **Newport Beach**. When you reach Newport Boulevard, you'll turn right and eventually merge onto Balboa Boulevard towards the **Balboa Peninsula**. Follow the signs to the **Balboa Island Ferry** (www.balboaislandferry.com). The ferry has provided continuous service between Balboa Island and the Peninsula since 1919.

Turn off the motor, step out of your car, and enjoy the four-minute ride across the harbor to **Balboa Island**. The ride costs a whopping $1.50 for both car and driver, plus a nominal fee for additional passengers.

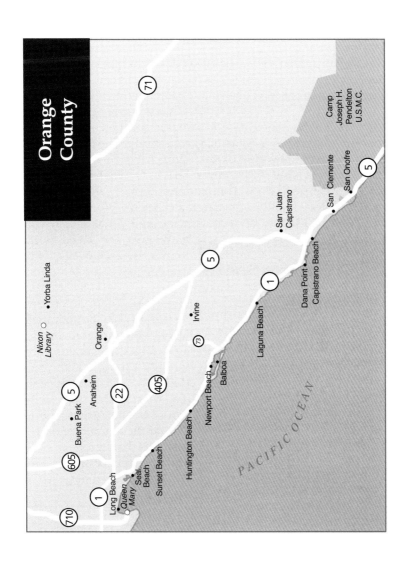

Orange County

Nixon Library
Yorba Linda
Buena Park
Anaheim
Orange
Long Beach
Queen Mary
Seal Beach
Sunset Beach
Huntington Beach
Newport Beach
Balboa
Irvine
Laguna Beach
Dana Point
Capistrano Beach
San Juan Capistrano
San Clemente
San Onofre
Camp Joseph H. Pendelton U.S.M.C.

PACIFIC OCEAN

710
1
605
5
22
405
73
5
1
5
71

Once you reach Balboa Island, you'll take Park Avenue to Marine Avenue, where the quaint village is located. Look for a parking spot and be mindful of any parking regulations, such as "permit only" or "street sweeping" hours. The island is extremely congested, so you may have to park a few blocks away. Stroll along **Marine Avenue** where a number of unique shops are located. Be sure to stop by **Dad's** about half-way down the block for a **Balboa Bar**, a chocolate or vanilla ice-cream bar dipped in a vat of chocolate than rolled in chocolate or rainbow sprinkles.

After you've spent some time on Balboa Island, hop in the car and continue down Marine Avenue, over the bridge and up the hill to Pacific Coast Highway. To your right, north of Pacific Coast Highway at Newport Center Drive, is **Fashion Island** (shopfashionisland.com). This outdoor shopping and entertainment complex is home to upscale retailers, such as **Bloomingdale's** and **Neiman Marcus**, as well as many individual shops. The walkways are laced with fountains, greenways, and unexpected amusements, such as a carousel and miniature train. There are many restaurants on the premises where you can grab lunch, including **Cheesecake Factory, PF Chang's**, and **Yard House**, as well as an eclectic food court located on the bottom level of the Atrium Court. During the summer months Fashion Island hosts an outdoor concert series on Wednesday evenings that is free to the public.

After leaving Fashion Island, continue south along Pacific Coast Highway. After crossing MacArthur Boulevard you'll happen upon the charming hamlet of **Corona**

Botanical Gardens

If you decide to stop in Corona del Mar on your tour of the coastal cities, consider stopping by the **Sherman Library and Gardens**, a 2.2 acre horticultural retreat. This oasis, located within misting distance of the sea, features a wonderful gallery of botanical collections. There is a cactus garden, an outdoor tea garden, and a lovely rose garden and tropical conservatory. There is a café on the premises, too. *Info:* www.slgardens.org. Tel. 949/ 673-1880. Corona del Mar. Open daily from 10am-4pm. Admission adults $3, children $1.

del Mar, which is actually part of Newport Beach. You can stop for a while and walk around, or continue on for another 10 minutes to **Laguna Beach**. Look for a place to park either along Broadway or Forest Avenue where there are municipal lots that don't

cost much, otherwise be prepared to feed the meters on a regular basis.

The corner art gallery is as commonplace in Laguna Beach as the mini-mall is in other communities. You'll discover nearly 100 galleries where a variety of art forms are on continuous display, from plein-air paintings to striking objects d'art to creative photographic works. **North Laguna Beach** is home to the historic **Gallery Row**, located along the 300 and 400 blocks of North Coast Highway. More than 20 galleries, such as the Lu Martin Galleries and Peter Blake Gallery, display a collection of original art. The **California Art Gallery** specializes in Early California Impressionists and watercolor artists from 1925-1950, while Native American art and artifacts are found at **Len Wood's Indian Territory, Inc**. The artists that convene at **Studio 7** are a talented group of plein-air impressionists who capture local land and seascapes on canvas.

ALTERNATIVE PLAN

Skip one of the beach cities and visit **Mission at San Juan Capistrano** instead. The grounds will give you a sense of the history amid the fabled arches, Moorish Fountains, Indian burial grounds, ruins of a stone church, soldiers' barracks and 10-acre garden. On the last Saturday of the month the mission hosts **Living History Days**, where costumed docents lead demonstrations in such time-forgotten skills as wool spinning and panning for gold. *Info:* www.missionsjc.com. Tel. 949/234-1300. San Juan Capistrano. Ortega Highway and Camino Capistrano. Open daily 8:30am-5pm. Admission adults $7, children $5.

Downtown streets are also lined with shops and restaurants. You'll want to stroll Broadway, Forest, Gleneyre and Coast Highway if you're in search of unique treasures. As the sun begins to set, head over to **Las Brisas** at 361 Cliff Drive overlooking the ocean. Request a patio table, order a trademark margarita, and enjoy the sunset. If you prefer to sit indoors, ask for a table by the window. For dinner, you'll want to dine at one of Laguna Beach's waterfront restaurants. My top choices are **The Loft** or **The Studio** both at the Montage Resort and Spa, **Splashes** at the Surf and Sand Resort, or **The Beach House** restaurant. If you want to hang with the locals and vacationing celebrities, head to **230 Forest Avenue** in town *(see Orange County Best Sleeps & Eats).*

A FANTASTIC ORANGE COUNTY WEEKEND

A weekend in Orange County will give you plenty of time to prowl the shopping venues, visit one or two significant museums, and spend some time relaxing at the **beach**. You can also use a day to visit either **Disneyland Resort** or **Knott's Berry Farm.**

Friday Evening
Take in a performance at the **Laguna Playhouse**, which was launched in a living room in 1920 and has grown to one of the most respectable performing arts venues in the state. Many well-known actors have taken to the stage, and an unknown Harrison Ford caught the attention of audience members when he performed in *John Brown's Body* in 1965. *Info:* www.lagunaplayhouse.org. Tel. 949/497-ARTS. Laguna Beach. At the Moulton Theater. 606 Laguna Canyon Road.

After the play, stop at the **Hotel Laguna's Terrace Restaurant** for a drink and great views of the Pacific. *Info:* www.hotellaguna.com. Tel. 949/494-1151. 425 South Coast Highway.

Saturday
Wake up, draw back the curtains and get ready to start your day.

Take a walk along the beach before the crowds arrive, then head to breakfast where the locals dine at **Zinc Café & Market**. The café draws a loyal crowd for full breakfasts or just lattes and scones. *Info:* www.zinccafe.com. Tel. 949/494-6302. 350 Ocean Avenue.

After breakfast, walk up to the **Laguna Art Museum**. Founded in 1918 by a small ensemble of artists, the Laguna Art Museum is the oldest cultural institution in the area. Its permanent collection holds more than 5,000 works from California artists spanning from the early 19th century to the present day. *Info:* www.lagunaartmuseum.org, Tel. 949/494-8971. 307 Cliff Drive.

From the museum, it's on to the tasting room at Orange County's only winery. Meet the winemaker at **Laguna Canyon Winery**, and enjoy tasting the latest vintage crushed, pressed and bottled on the premises. The winery is located in Laguna Canyon, hence the name. *Info:* www.lagunacanyonwinery.com. Tel. 949/715-9463. 2133 Laguna Canyon Road. Tastings start at $2 each. Taste any five wines, purchase a bottle, and the fee is waived.

Head back to your hotel room, perhaps with a bottle of wine purchased on your outing, and enjoy the rest of the evening on your oceanfront balcony.

Take a Cooking Class!

If you like to cook, enroll at a cooking class at the renowned **Laguna Culinary Arts**. The school's kitchen is nestled in Laguna Canyon near the grounds of the Sawdust Festival. Courses are geared towards the home chef with a wide variety of hands-on classes with a full spectrum of cuisines and cooking styles. Saturday evening classes are offered from 5-9pm. If you're visiting the last Saturday of the month, be sure to check out the Saturday Afternoon Tasting Room from 1-4pm. One dollar buys you a taste of eight wines selected from a wide selection of domestic and international vintages. *Info:* www.lagunaculinaryarts.com. Tel. 949/494-0745. 845 Laguna Canyon Rd.

Sunday

Even if you're not an active church goer, you may still enjoy a service at the **Crystal Cathedral**. Designed by Philip Johnson, the cathedral resembles a four-pointed star and boasts 10,000 panes of glass that cover the web-like, transparent walls and ceilings. The church, founded by Dr. Robert Schuller, is one of Orange County's most notable architectural landmarks. Sunday morning services are held at 9:25am and 11:05am. *Info:* www.crystalcathedral.org. Tel. 714/971-4000. Garden Grove. 12141 Lewis Street.

ALTERNATIVE PLAN

If your main purpose for coming to Orange County is to visit **Disneyland**, you'll need to allow for almost the entire weekend. I recommend you book a room at one of the Disney hotels (*see Orange County Sleeps & Eats*) and allow yourself both days to visit Disneyland, Disney's California Adventure, and Downtown Disney. Contact Disneyland Resort to see what vacation packages are available that include both accommodations and admission to the theme parks.

If the Crystal Cathedral is not for you, then head to **Bowers Museum** near downtown Santa Ana. This world-class, internationally celebrated institution of art and culture features a half-dozen exhibits with two unique gallery stores. Collections include tribal beauty, plein air paintings from renowned California artists, Native American art, and Pre-Columbian art. Plan to have lunch at **Tangata**, the museum's courtyard restaurant, featuring an assortment of tapas, sandwiches, and salads. *Info:* www.bowersmuseum.org. Tel. 714/567-3600. Santa Ana. Open Tuesday-Sunday 10am-4pm. Admission adults $19, children $14.

Maybe you don't want to head inland and would prefer to spend the rest of your time near the coast. In that case, skip both the Crystal Cathedral and Bowers Museum and head to **Duffy Boat Rentals** in Newport Beach. You'll be the captain of your own electric boat out on the open and tame waters of Newport Harbor. Each vessel, which is easy to navigate, has window enclosures in case the weather is a bit chilly. Bring your favorite foods and beverages, and enjoy a floating picnic. *Info:* www.duffyboats.com. Tel. 949/645-6812. Newport Beach. 2001 W. Coast Highway.

Spend the rest of your Sunday afternoon at **South Coast Plaza**. Housed in two buildings joined together by an elongated, arched bridge, this is a shoppers' paradise. In the main building you'll find every designer represented, all the major jewelers, and up-

See a Pro Game!

Don't miss a chance to catch an **Angels baseball game** if you're visiting anytime from April-October. Games are played at Angel Stadium just off the 57 freeway at Katella – about 10 minutes from Disneyland. On the other side of the Freeway at the Ball Road exit is the Honda Center where the **Anaheim Ducks** go puck-to-puck during hockey season, which takes place October through April.

scale department stores anchoring the plethora of wings. The smaller annex, formerly known as Crystal Court, is where most of the home furnishing stores are located: Pottery Barn, Restoration Hardware, Z Gallery and so on. There are plenty of dining options throughout with some very upscale freestanding restaurants located around the perimeter of the mall as well as at South Coast Plaza's sister center **South Coast Village**. *Info:* www.southcoastplaza.com. Tel. 714/435-2000. Santa Ana. 3333 Bristol Street. Open daily from 10am.

A WONDERFUL WEEK IN ORANGE COUNTY

You came, you saw, you conquered! It's possible to do it all with a week in Orange County and still feel as if you haven't been rushed. You'll be able to visit **Disneyland Resort**, spend a day or more at the **beach**, travel to **Catalina Island** just 26 miles across the sea and, who knows, maybe even learn to surf.

RECOMMENDED PLAN: You'll want to spend some significant time at the **beach** communities, as well as allow for a day, maybe even two, at **Disneyland Resort**. Take another day to spend at the **Richard Nixon Library and Birthplace** in the northern part of the county, and a few hours strolling around the historic **Orange Circle**. A week also gives you enough time for a daytrip to **Catalina Island**.

Anaheim-Disneyland Resort

Touted as the Happiest Place on Earth, Disneyland Resort now features two theme parks and an open-air dining and entertainment complex. The original is always the best, so if you only have one day to spend do not, I repeat, do not waste your time trying to visit both parks because, when you factor in the lines, meals and entertainment options, you're going to feel hurried. Instead, visit the original **Disneyland** and forgo Disney's California Adventure. As you cross through the gates into the **Magic Kingdom**, your first encounter will be **Main Street, USA**. The street is lined with shops and restaurant, and at the end is Sleeping Beauty's Castle, as well as various pathways heading in all directions to

the different themed lands: Fanstasyland, Adventureland, Tomorrowland, New Orleans Square, Frontierland, Critter Country, and Mickey's Toontown.

Across the promenade is the resort's newer park, **Disney's California Adventure**, which celebrates the fun and sun of the Golden State like only Disney can. The park includes a unique beachfront area, a Hollywood-esque district, and an area paying homage to the state's natural

Calling Mickey...

Disneyland receives more than **7 million phone calls** a year. The bulk of callers want to speak to Mickey Mouse.

beauty. The rides tend to be a bit more adventurous and hair-raising than those at Disneyland. Both theme parks feature entertainment throughout the day, parades, strolling characters and, in the summer months, a fantastic fireworks show.

Downtown Disney, which is a free attraction and built to look like a city center in a Disneyesque way, is located outside the entrance to both theme parks. My recommendation is to eat at one of Downtown Disney's restaurants instead of inside the park. You'll find the food to be much more satisfying than the fast food kiosks inside the parks. Also, any one of the restaurants inside the three resort hotels are also good, alternative options *(see Orange County Sleeps & Eats). Info:* www.disneyland.com. Tel. 714/781.4565. Anaheim. 1313 Harbor Boulevard. Hours and prices vary, call ahead.

Disneyland and California Adventure both offer **Fast Pass** for the most popular rides. You simply go to the attraction and look for the Fast Pass sign. You'll give the Fast Pass machine your admission ticket, and the machine will give you a ticket with a specific time frame in which to return to the ride. It can sometimes be several hours later, but then you're free to roam the park. When you return you're ushered to the front of the line. There is no charge for a Fast Pass, it's simply a convenient service Disney offers.

Buena Park

If you want to visit a theme park where the rides are a bit more stomach churning, then skip Disneyland and head to nearby **Knotts Berry Farm** in Buena Park, billed as America's first theme park. It began when Walter Knott and his wife Virginia operated a chicken restaurant and 20-acre berry farm during the 1930s. By 1940, the restaurant was serving more than 4,000 Sunday dinners with lines wrapped

around the building. In order to placate their hungry customers, Walter developed Ghost Town, the first of Knott's Berry Farm's themed areas.

Knott's has several theme areas, including the original Ghost Town, offering a mix of everything from mild to wild. The Boardwalk, Wild Water Wilderness and Fiesta Village all contain a mix of semi-tame and extreme rides, many not for the faint of heart. Only **Camp Snoopy**, which is geared towards younger children, offers very kid-friendly options. Throughout the day there are shows and demonstrations to enjoy. Knott's Marketplace, located adjacent to the theme park, is a free area where you can shop and dine at **Mrs. Knott's Chicken Dinner Restaurant**. A replica of Independence Hall is also located at the Marketplace and shows are held daily that bring history to life.

Knott's Berry Farm also operates **Soak City** from Memorial Day to Labor Day. This water park, located next to the theme park, is a great place to cool off on a hot summer day. There are several pool areas and water rides. Wear your swimsuit and layer on the SPF. *Info:* www.knotts.com. Buena Park. Tel. 714/220-5200. 8039 Beach Boulevard. Call for hours and admission prices.

If you're visiting the area during the month of October, you'll want to visit Knott's Berry Farm annual **Halloween Haunt**. For more than 30 years, the park has undergone a major transformation to become **Knott's Scary Farm**. The thrills get underway after dark as monsters and ghouls roam the park – it's one of Southern California's most popular Halloween attractions. A separate admission price is required, and the event often sells out weeks in advance. Not recommended for young children.

Don't Miss ...

• some time on the beach
• a day at **Disneyland**
• **Nixon Library & Birthplace**
• the historic **Orange Circle**
• a daytrip to **Catalina Island**

Orange

East of Anaheim and Buena Park is the **Orange Circle** in **Old Town Orange**. Consisting of a perfect square mile divided into equally perfect quarters, the circle features an oval plaza with a fountain as its center. The roads labeled *"street"* run north and south, those labeled *"avenue"* run east and west. If you visit, you'll feel as if you're stepping back in time. Most of the buildings and storefronts are original 19th and early 20th century structures. Shopping here is fun because the stores are one-of-a-kind with a high concentration of antique dealers. There are also some nice restaurants along the circle, as well as great pubs and tearooms located on the four spokes that jut from the circle. Be sure to pay a visit to **Watson's Drugs and Soda Fountain** on East Chapman, which was established in 1899 and is an authentic relic from the past. Many movies have also been filmed in and around the Orange Circle, including *That Thing You Do* starring Tom Hanks. *Info:* Exit the 57 Freeway at Chapman near Angel Stadium and head east. The Orange Circle is about a mile up the road.

Up in the hills of Orange is **Arden-The Helena Modjeska Historic House and Gardens** where European stage actress Helena

Food Treats in the OC

Don't leave The OC without having treated your taste buds to one of these...

- A **Balboa Bar** at Dad's on Balboa Island
- A **Date Shake** at the historic Ruby's Shake Shack along Pacific Coast Highway
- An **OC Martini** at the lobby lounge inside the Montage Resort & Spa in Laguna Beach.
- A **slice of boysenberry pie** at Mrs. Knott's Chicken Dinner Restaurant outside of Knott's Berry Farm
- A classic **cheeseburger** from In-n-Out, the ultimate California burger since 1948...look for the trademark yellow arrows pointing down to the restaurants' red and white buildings. Several locations throughout the county.

Modjeska built her secluded canyon home after retiring from the theater. You can visit the rustic home, situated on a 10,000-acre parcel, by advance reservation only. It's a unique outing that takes you through the years that Modjeska resided in the canyon home. *Info:* You'll need to call to make a reservations as tours are only held four times a month. Tel. 949/923-2230. Admission $5 per person.

Yorba Linda-Nixon Library
Located about 15 minutes from Disneyland is Yorba Linda and **The Richard Nixon Library & Birthplace**. This northern Orange County town first gained international attention when the library opened in 1990 and again when the press converged on the town to cover the funeral of the 37th president. You can visit the nine-acre complex, which currently is the only United States presidential library built and maintained exclusively through private funds, every day of the week except for holidays when the library is closed. Best described as a three-dimensional walk-through memoir, highlights include a 52,000-square-foot museum, 22 high-tech galleries, movie and interactive video theaters, and the spectacular First Lady's Garden.

Lunch at PJ's

Make a point to have lunch at **PJ's Abbey**. Housed in an 1891 Gothic-style Victorian Baptist Church, the setting and menu are unique. The restaurant also serves a fabulous Sunday brunch. *Info:* www.pjsabbey.com Tel. 714/771-8556. Orange. 182 S. Orange Street. Open for lunch, dinner and Sunday brunch. Closed Monday.

Be sure to pay a visit to President Nixon's fully restored birthplace, his childhood home built by his father the year before he was born, and the flower-circlet memorial sites of the both the President and Mrs. Nixon. The library also hosts many special events and guest speakers throughout the year, so be sure to check the website before you plan your visit. *Info:* www.nixonfoundation.org. Tel. 714/993-3393. Yorba Linda. 18001 Yorba Linda Boulevard. Open Monday-Saturday 10am-5pm, Sunday 11am-5pm. Admission adults $9.95, children $3.75.

Mission San Juan Capistrano
If you feel like you've had your fill of the surf and sand, you can alter your One Great Day by skipping one of the beach cities and including **Mission at San Juan Capistrano** as part of your agenda. Established November 1, 1776, this is the seventh of the 21 California missions founded by Father Junipero Serra. As with all the missions it was the Indians that were recruited, rarely by choice, to construct the buildings. The sound of the century-old bells will guide you to the grounds where you'll get a  sense of the history amid the fabled arches, Moorish Fountains, Indian burial grounds, ruins of a stone church, soldier's barracks and 10-acre garden. On the last Saturday of the month the mission hosts **Living History Days**, where costumed docents lead demonstrations in such time-forgotten skills as wool spinning and panning for gold. *Info:* www.missionsjc.com. Tel.949/ 234-1300. San Juan Capistrano. Ortega Highway and Camino Capistrano. Open daily 8:30am-5pm. Admission adults $7, children $5.

If you're visiting Orange County in mid-March, you can take part in the annual **Return of the Swallows Festival** at the Mission San Juan Capistrano. For nearly 100 years, like clockwork, hundreds of swallows return to the mission to nest on or near St. Joseph's Day, March 19. Each year the entire town marks their return with a three-day celebration.

The Beach Cities
In Orange County, life really is a beach. Every traveler needs some down time, so you'll want to spend yours lounging on the sand or taking part in an activity that requires some sand beneath your feet and a even layer of sunscreen.

The beach cities begin near the LA County line in **Seal Beach**, a sleepy town with a Main Street of shops, restaurants and pubs. At the end of Main Street is Seal Beach with a beachfront playground and landmark pier. As you work your way down **Pacific Coast Highway**, the road that links all the seaside cities together like a strand of pearls, you'll pass through **Sunset Beach** before coming upon **Bolsa Chica State Beach** at the corner of Warner Avenue in **Huntington Beach**. To your left is the **Bolsa Chica Ecological Reserve** and to your right is the beach.

Further down the road is **Huntington City Beach,** located between Seapoint Avenue and Beach Boulevard, and past that is **Huntington State Beach**, which continues to the Santa Ana River. **Downtown Huntington Beach**, at the corner of Main Street and Pacific Coast Highway, is where the city's 20-block shopping, dining and entertainment area begins. The outdoor **Surfers' Hall of Fame** and the **Surfing Walk of Fame** are located here, and just up the road is the **International Surfing Museum** featuring displays of surfing memorabilia, a camera used to film the movie *Endless Summer* and other artifacts. *Info:* www.surfingmuseum.org. Tel. 714/960-3483. Huntington Beach. 411 Olive Street. Open daily noon-5pm. Free.

Beach Bonfire

A **bonfire** on the beach is a rite of passage in Southern California and a favorite year-round pastime. **Bolsa Chica State Beach** has hundreds of cement fire rings that are available on a first come, first-served basis. Wood and sundries can purchased at any nearby grocery store. Be warned, the fire rings are highly coveted on summer and holiday weekends so try to plan your bonfire for a weekday evening.

Next, as you continue south down Pacific Coast Highway, you'll come upon the swanky seaside town of **Newport Beach,** known for its multimillion-dollar homes, expensive yachts, fabulous beaches, designer boutiques and fast cars. You can also get back to nature at **The Environmental Nature Center** where guided walking tours are offered among the 2 1/2 acre wildlife preserve. There are 13 California plant communities, trail guides, and Orange County's only Butterfly House were several species native to the county are found. *Info:* www.encenter.org. Tel. 949/645-8489. 1601 16th Street. Open Monday-Friday 8am-5pm, until 4pm on Saturday.

Stop by **Roger's Gardens** near Fashion Island, a landmark nursery that is as much of an attraction as anything in these parts. During the holidays, its lavish display of lights and decorations rivals any paid

Best OC Beach Activities

- Play **beach volleyball**
- Go **biking** along the oceanfront strand
- Enroll in a local **surf school**
- Have a **bonfire** after dark
- take part in the seasonal **grunion hunt**
- Master the art of **body surfing**
- Cast a **fishing** line from a jetty
- **Stroll** along the sand
- Go **in-line skating** along the oceanfront strand

attraction. Weekly lectures and events, with topics such as Citrus Tasting or Landscape Design Trends, are free and in high demand. *Info:* www.rogersgardens.com. Tel. 949/640-5800. 2301 San Joaquin Hills.

Newport Beach is also home to five beaches, if you count **Corona del Mar State Beach** and **Little Corona del Mar State Beach**, which begin at the foot of Jasmine Avenue and Ocean Boulevard. The other three beaches are Newport Beach, which parallels Newport Boulevard until it becomes **Balboa Beach** along the Peninsula, and **West Jetty View Park**, better known as "The Wedge" because of its slice of daring surf at the end of the peninsula.

Laguna Beach
Continuing along Pacific Coast Highway, you'll next arrive in **Laguna Beach**. Just north of town is **Crystal Cove State Park** where historic cottages are available for rent *(see Orange County Sleeps & Eats)*. Enter at Pelican Point, Los Trancos, Reef Point or

 El Moro Canyon. **The Coves**: Shaw's, Fisherman's and Diver's are a trio of hidden inlets laid out along Cliff Drive. Make your way down the jagged ridge to discover tide pool pouches, excellent surf and a secluded setting. There are lifeguards on duty, but no other conveniences to speak of. Access Fairview Street for Shaw's Cove, and the 600 block of Cliff Drive for the other two.

Main Beach, at Coast Highway and Broadway, is perhaps the most popular if not crowded stretch of sand. A single lifeguard beacon sits elevated above all the activity as swimmers frolic in the water, while a friendly game of hoops creates temporary gridlock from the cars making their way down Coast Highway. The swimming is good, and the offshore **Laguna Beach Marine Life Refuge** makes for pristine diving conditions. Walk south along the beach and you'll happen upon **Street Beaches**, which are shielded from the road, and further down is **Arch Cove**, where fabulous homes cling to the hillside. Both beaches are manned by lifeguards and ideal for swimming.

Along the 31300 block of Coast Highway in South Laguna is **Aliso Creek County Beach** where there is a contemporary fishing pier and a hidden cove to the south. The beach also has volleyball nets and lifeguards on duty. Just past this beach is **Thousand Steps**, one of the area's most popular beaches. The name comes from the long, steep staircase that leads down to the surf and sand below.

If you're visiting during the months of July or August, a visit to the **Pageant of the Masters** is a must. The 74-year-old celebration of art in "living pictures" or *tableaux vivants*, is certainly one of the nation's premiere art events. Ordinary people, volunteers actually, are cast in incredible roles that faithfully recreate classical and contemporary works of art costumed and posed to look exactly like their counterparts in the original pieces. The event is held outdoors in Laguna Canyon with a complete professional orchestra, original score, live narration, intricate sets, and sophisticated lighting. A night at the Pageant of the Masters is by all means a happening. Visit the website to order your tickets in advance. *Info:* www.foapom.com. Tel. 800/487-3387. Laguna Beach. 650 Laguna Canyon Road. Shows are at 8:30pm nightly during July and August. Tickets start at $20 per person.

The **Sawdust Festival**, another annual summer happening that shouldn't be missed, takes place during the same time as Pageant of the Masters. You're invited to shop along sawdust-covered paths and prowl outdoor booths where only local artists (you must live or have a studio in Laguna Beach) can display their works. Check out the demo booths, hands-on workshops, children's art booth and live entertainment. Visit the festival in the evening when the canyon is a bit cooler and the twinkle lights are aglow. *Info:* www.sawdustfestival.org. Tel. 949/494-3030. Laguna Beach. 935 Laguna Canyon Road. Open late June through Labor Day daily 10am-10pm. Admission adults $7, children $3.

Dana Point

Dana Point neighbors Laguna Beach and boasts a fabulous harbor and marina, as well as a pair of beaches. **Salt Creek Beach Park**, just below the Ritz-Carlton Resort, offers a bisection of half-mile beaches. The resort is considered the division point and to the south is Dana Strand. The crowds are modest and the swimming safe. South of Salt Creek Beach, below the Laguna Cliffs Marriott Resort, is **Doheny State Beach**. This is a great place to learn how to surf because the waves are so mellow. You'll also find an expansive greenbelt area for picnicking, as well as beach rentals, volleyball courts and other public facilities.

Further south, past Doheny State Beach, is family-friendly **Capistrano Beach Park** in San Juan Capistrano and, near the San Diego County line, **San Clemente City Beach** in the town by the same name. **San Clemente State Beach** is the furthest beach south in Orange County.

Catalina Island

With an entire week to spend in Orange County, set aside a day to travel to Catalina Island. The **Catalina Flyer** departs several times daily from the Balboa Pavilion in Newport Beach near the end of the Balboa Peninsula.

For the most part, Catalina is a best-kept secret enjoyed mostly by the local mainlanders. It was first developed in the 1920s by chewing gum mogul William Wrigley. He owned both the island and the Chicago Cubs, who would come here for spring training. His former estate sits perched high on a hill and is now a luxury bed and breakfast inn.

Avalon is the only developed town on the island. **Crescent Avenue**, which runs along the waterfront, serves as the town's main street and is brimming with quaint shops, outdoor cafes and small inns. You're likely going to notice very few cars on the island, and that's because this is the only California city authorized by the State Legislature to regulate the number and size of vehicles allowed to putter about its streets. Currently, there is an 8-10 year wait to bring a car on the island and most people are more than eager to walk, bicycle or use a golf cart to get around.

At the end of Crescent Avenue is a large, round building. This is the historic **Casino**, once abuzz with social events, it now houses a museum and the island's only movie theater and ballroom. The vintage 1909 **Green Pleasure Pier**, which stretches out into the snug harbor, is a favorite spot to fish. Even though the island is small, it isn't lacking any recreation. You can golf, snorkel, scuba dive, ride horseback, rent boats and kayaks, fish, and hike. You will also find some cultural and historic diversions, such as home tours of the unique Holly Hill House and casino. The **Wrigley Memorial and Botanical Gardens** is dedicated to preserving the island's bountiful plant life.

The remote **Two Harbors**, located at the island's isthmus, is popular among campers. There is a bed and breakfast inn, one restaurant, two harbors (hence the name) and a small market. *Info:* For ferry transportation and island information, contact the Catalina Island Chamber of Commerce. www.catalinachamber.com. Tel. 310/510-1520.

If your plans include an overnight getaway to Catalina Island there are a number of lodging choices available. I highly recommend the **Inn on Mt. Ada**, the extremely luxurious former Wrigley estate, but if you would prefer not to splurge, see Catalina Island in Chapter 9, *Best Sleeps & Eats*.

6. SANTA BARBARA

If you enjoy glistening beaches, sidewalk cafes, an unforgettable glass of wine, and stylish boutiques then you'll certainly be smitten with **Santa Barbara**. Its distinct architecture is the perfect blend of Mediterranean, Spanish Colonial, early California, Monterey, Moorish, Islamic and the occasional Victorian vestige. Santa Barbara is often compared to the European Riviera. The two regions share an enviable climate due to their south-facing positions, and both are sheltered between mountains and islands. Each has its share of celebrity residents. While there is a Hollywood element in these parts, the town is void of any tinsel or tabloid fodder.

The pace is unhurried here, whether you're window shopping along **State Street** or motoring along the **Santa Ynez wine trail** in search of the perfect pinot noir. The resorts are posh, but never pretentious. Restaurants run the gamut from delicious dives to more sophisticated eateries. There are many landmarks, historic attractions, museums, and family venues worth exploring. No matter how lengthy your visit, it won't seem long enough.

ONE GREAT DAY IN SANTA BARBARA

I can almost guarantee that you'll feel cheated if you only spend a day in Santa Barbara, but if time is of the essence you can still make the most of your 24 hours. You'll want to explore **downtown** and the **beach area**, do a little wine tasting in town, visit the **historic mission**, walk along **Stearns Wharf** and find time for some memorable meals.

Chances are your hotel or inn provided you with morning coffee and a continental breakfast. In some cases, you may have even been treated to a full-fledge meal as many of the resorts and inns offer this complimentary to their guests. In the event that this wasn't the case, start your day with breakfast at **Pierre Lafond Bistro** on State Street *(see Santa Barbara Sleep & Eats)*. The restaurant is casual with gourmet offerings, such as creative omelets, breakfast sandwiches, and morning burritos. If you're thinking of heading up towards the wine country, you can also pick up a picnic lunch.

After breakfast, maybe with a cup of joe in hand, take the self-guided **Red Tile Walking Tour**. This tour will give you an appreciation for Santa Barbara's rich architecture and, at the same time, familiarize you with downtown. Maps are available at many locations around town, including the **Visitors Center** on the corner of Cabrillo Avenue and Garden Street across from the beach and Chase Palm Park. The walking tour starts at the **Santa Barbara Courthouse** at 1100 Anacapa Street at Anapamu, which gained some notoriety during the Michael Jackson trial back in the early 1990s. Free guided tours of the courthouse are conducted Monday-Saturday, but you can explore this magnificent Spanish-Moorish structure on your own. Go to the top and

enjoy the rooftop views from the tower, and be sure to bring your camera. On your tour you'll also visit some of the town's historic buildings, including adobe structures, quaint shopping arcades, and the famed Presidio as well as some notable venues, such as the **Santa Barbara Museum of Art** and the **Lobero Theater**, built in 1873 and still used today.

Next, take a drive up to the **Mission Santa Barbara**, the "Queen" of the California missions. The mission, the 10th in the 21 mission

chain, was founded by Father Junipero Serra in 1786. The structure was built by Chumash Indians who resided at the mission and were trained by the Spaniards in agriculture and animal husbandry. During its 200-year history, the mission has suffered damage on two occasions when earthquakes struck the region in 1812 and 1925. It is the only mission of its kind with twin bell towers, and its stone façade was inspired by an ancient Latin temple during pre-Christian Rome. The mission remains a place of worship for Catholic parishioners, and the complex includes a small museum, courtyard gardens, cemetery and gift shops. *Info:* www.sbmission.org. Tel. 805/682-4149. North of Downtown. 2201 Laguna Street. Open daily 9am-5pm. Admission $4 – the outside grounds and gift shop are free.

Head to Stearns Wharf at the foot of State Street and have lunch at the **Harbor Restaurant** *(see Santa Barbara Best Sleeps & Eats)* located right on the pier. Request a window booth overlooking the water. Upstairs is **Longboard's**, a more casual bar and grille with outdoor tables and great ocean views. The food isn't as good, but it's fine for appetizers, sandwiches, burgers or salads.

With only a day in Santa Barbara, there's no time to hit the wine trail and do it justice. So, instead, do a little **wine tasting in town**.

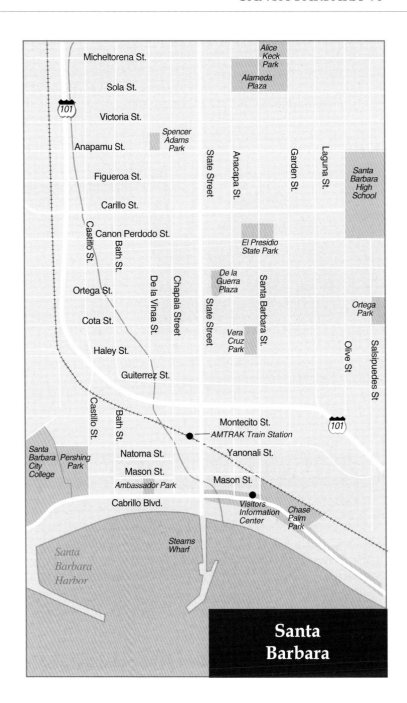

Micheltorena St.

Alice Keck Park

Sola St.

Alameda Plaza

101

Victoria St.

Spencer Adams Park

Anapamu St.

State Street

Anacapa St.

Garden St.

Laguna St.

Santa Barbara High School

Figueroa St.

Carillo St.

Castillo St.

Canon Perdodo St.

Bath St.

El Presidio State Park

Ortega St.

De la Vinaa St.

Chapala Street

De la Guerra Plaza

Santa Barbara St.

Cota St.

State Street

Ortega Park

Vera Cruz Park

Haley St.

Guiterrez St.

Olive St.

Salsipuedes St

Castillo St.

Bath St.

Montecito St.

101

AMTRAK Train Station

Santa Barbara City College

Pershing Park

Natoma St.

Yanonali St.

Mason St.

Ambassador Park

Mason St.

Cabrillo Blvd.

Visitors Information Center

Chase Palm Park

Stearns Wharf

Santa Barbara Harbor

Santa Barbara

East Beach Wine Company (201 South Milpas) and **Stearns Wharf Vintners** (at the end of the wharf) both pour several different Santa Barbara wines with many vintages hailing from smaller producers who do not have tasting rooms at their vineyards. **Santa Barbara Winery** (202 Anacapa Street), part of Lafond Vineyards in the Santa Ynez Valley, has its tasting room in an industrial area just north of the waterfront.

 Afterwards, head back to State Street and do some window-shopping. Stroll through **La Arcada** where in the very back is the **Acapulco Mexican Restaurant** (1114 State Street). Ask for a table on the fountain courtyard that fronts the restaurant and order a blended margarita, but skip the food. Located across the street near Paseo Nuevo is the incredibly popular **Pascucci's** (see Santa Barbara Best Eats) where you can request one of the curtained booths, order a glass of locally produced cabernet, and savor ample-sized plates of pasta all without breaking the bank.

A FANTASTIC SANTA BARBARA WEEKEND

A weekend in Santa Barbara is a celebration of romance and fine living. You'll have time to spend in town and along the **waterfront**, a day to venture up to the **wine country**, and a few hours to take in some key attractions. If you're traveling with kids, there are plenty of places that both you and your little ones will enjoy.

Friday Night
Check in to the **Simpson House Inn** *(see Santa Barbara Best*

Sleeps & Eats). If you arrive in the late afternoon, you'll be welcomed by a gourmet spread that, if not careful, will spoil your appetite. The wine country cuisine, presented in a casual buffet-style with a selection of local wines, easily rivals any restaurant in town. If you arrive later, unpack and head down to State Street and enjoy dinner at **Café Buenos Aires** *(see Santa Barbara Best Sleeps & Eats)* for some Argentine-inspired fare and entertainment. If the weather is nice, request a table on the outdoor patio.

After dinner, you can stroll along State Street or take in a movie at the historic **Arlington Theater** across the street from Café Buenos Aires. The 1931 Mission Revival theater is a grand movie palace that shows first run movies on a single screen. Tickets are still purchased at the free-standing ticket booth under the marquee. You'll walk through the Spanish courtyard and past a fountain to enter the lobby. The auditorium resembles a Spanish village with faux lanterns, curtained windows and iron staircases that lead to nowhere. The ceiling is filled with twinkling stars, giving you, the movie goer, the odd sensation that you're watching the film outdoors.

The theater also doubles as a performing arts venue, so there may not be a movie showing during your visit. If you want to experi-

Best SB Freebies

• Tour the **Santa Barbara Winery**
• Visit the **Santa Barbara Orchid Estate**
• See the historic stage coach stop at **Cold Springs Tavern**
• Visit the historical painted caves at **Chumash Painted Cave**
• Play in a pick-up game of volleyball at **East Beach** on Cabrillo Boulevard
• Listen to live concerts in **Chase Palm Park** and **Alameda Park**, June through August.
• Take a tour of the breathtaking **Santa Barbara Courthouse**
• Go tide pooling during low tide along the rocky area of **Leadbetter Beach**
• Birdwatch at the **Andree Clark Bird Refuge**
• Prowl the weekly **Sunday Arts & Crafts Fair** near Stearns Wharf

ence Santa Barbara's nightlife which, when compared to other towns, is almost non-existent, head to **Rocks** (801 State Street) for lemon-drop martinis and an energetic bar scene. **The James Joyce** (513 State Street) features live jazz on Friday evenings, or head to the upstairs lounge at **Blue Agave** (20 E. Cota Street).

Saturday
After breakfast, spend a little time at the inn enjoying the gardens and reading the paper before getting in the car and driving to the **Santa Barbara Wine Country**. You'll head north on State Street, which leads to Upper State Street. Look for the signs leading to Highway 154, where you'll veer off to the right. Just follow Highway 154 for about 40 minutes. On your way up, stop by the **Chumash Painted Cave** off Highway 154 at Painted Caves Road. Religious drawings by the Chumash Indians, as well as images of coastal fisherman dating back to the 1600s, are found in this sandstone cave. Take a few minutes here before pushing onward.

As you continue your drive along Highway 154, you'll see a sign for Grand Avenue, where the small town of **Los Olivos** is found. Continue on Highway 154 to Foxen Canyon Road where you'll encounter a number of stellar wineries. First is the **Firestone Vineyard,** where you'll turn left onto Zaca Station Road (Andrew Firestone, tire heir and best-known for being *The Bachelor*, belongs to the family that owns this winery). Back out on Foxen

Canyon Road is, in this order, **Curtis Winery**, **Fess Parker Winery**, **Zaca Mesa Winery** — my personal favorite — **Foxen Winery,** and **Rancho Sisquoc**.

Head back the way you came, passing all those tasting rooms you visited, and turn right on Grand Avenue, Los Olivos main road. There are several more tasting rooms located in town, including Andrew Murray Vineyards, Richard Longoria Wines, Los Olivos Vintners, Daniel Gehrs Wines, Kahn Winery, and Arthur Earl. Los Olivos Wine & Spirits Emporium, as well as Los Olivos Tasting

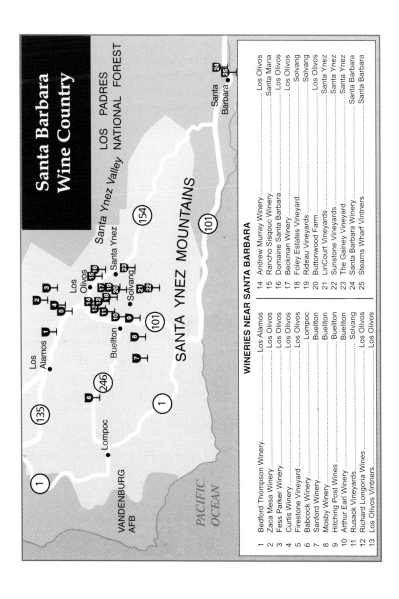

Santa Barbara Wine Country

PACIFIC OCEAN

VANDENBURG AFB

LOS PADRES NATIONAL FOREST

Santa Ynez Valley

Santa Ynez

SANTA YNEZ MOUNTAINS

Los Alamos

Los Olivos

Santa Ynez

Solvang

Buellton

Lompoc

Santa Barbara

WINERIES NEAR SANTA BARBARA

#	Winery	Location
1	Bedford Thompson Winery	Los Alamos
2	Zaca Mesa Winery	Los Olivos
3	Fess Parker Winery	Los Olivos
4	Curtis Winery	Los Olivos
5	Firestone Vineyard	Los Olivos
6	Babcock Winery	Lompoc
7	Sanford Winery	Buellton
8	Mosby Winery	Buellton
9	Hitching Post Wines	Buellton
10	Arthur Earl Winery	Buellton
11	Rusack Vineyards	Solvang
12	Richard Longoria Wines	Los Olivos
13	Los Olivos Vintners	Los Olivos
14	Andrew Murray Winery	Los Olivos
15	Rancho Sisquoc Winery	Santa Maria
16	Domaine Santa Barbara	Los Olivos
17	Beckman Winery	Los Olivos
18	Foley Estates Vineyard	Solvang
19	Rideau Vineyards	Solvang
20	Buttonwood Farm	Los Olivos
21	LinCourt Vineyards	Santa Ynez
22	Sunstone Vineyards	Santa Ynez
23	The Gainey Vineyard	Santa Ynez
24	Santa Barbara Winery	Santa Barbara
25	Stearns Wharf Vintners	Santa Barbara

Room and Wine Shop, and Los Olivos Wine Merchant, all specialize in hard-to-find wine acquisitions and tastings.

Stop in to the **Los Olivos Café** *(see Santa Barbara Best Sleeps & Eats)* for a fabulous lunch or take your food to go and enjoy a vineyard picnic at one of the wineries. If you take your lunch to go, then head back down to Highway 154 to Highway 246, which leads to Solvang. Stop at Gainey Vineyards (3950 East Highway 246), purchase a bottle of their award-winning wine, and enjoy lunch at a picnic table on the grounds.

If you enjoyed the movie *Sideways* as much as I did, you can request *Sideways The Map* from the Santa Barbara Convention & Visitors Bureau and take a self-driven tour on the same path forged by Miles and Jack as they celebrated Jack's final days as a bachelor. *Info:* Tel. 805/966-9222 or download a map at www.santabarbaraca.com.

Tour highlights include:
- **AJ Spurs** – where Miles and Jack meet waitress Cami
- **Days Inn Buellton** – the hotel where Miles and Jack stayed
- **Foxen Winery** – where the boys help themselves to full glasses of wine when the pourer turns her back
- **Sanford Winery** – where Miles attempts to enlighten Jack on the art of wine tasting

There are 18 memorable locations for movie buffs to visit. You can also request a free 34-page guide to many of the locations where movies, such as *Seabiscuit, Walk in the Clouds*, and *The Graduate* were filmed. *Info:* www.santabarbarafilmtour.com, or Tel. 800/676-1266.

After lunch, continue your journey along Highway 246 to **Solvang**. As you approach Solvang you'll see ostriches roaming freely behind a fence – this is **Ostrich Land**, which is open to the public and a favorite of kids. *Info:* 610 E. Highway 246.

Once you arrive in Solvang, park the car and walk the town. Settled by a group of Danes in 1911, Solvang has grown into a a

 kitschy attraction with its old world edifices, spinning windmills, and souvenir shops. There are several small inns, restaurants and bakeries – definitely make a point of having an *aebleskiver,* a Danish pancake-like treat. The **Mission Santa Ines**, built in 1804, is located nearby as well as the **Hans Christian Andersen Museum** where the writer's books, sketches and paper cutouts are on display. After you've spent some time wandering the streets, you'll enjoy a visit to **Nojoqui Falls** located about five miles south off Alisal Road and home to a magnificent 164-foot waterfall.

Take Alisal Road back to Highway 246 and turn left. You'll continue on through Solvang on to **Buellton** and take a turn onto Avenue of the Flags. At the corner is the landmark **Andersen's Pea Soup**, a restaurant that is nearing its 85th anniversary. What's so unique about this restaurant is not its décor, which is a bit outdated, nor the gift shop, which is a little tacky, but the rich, delicious pea soup. You'll want to stop here for dinner before heading back to Santa Barbara.

ALTERNATIVE PLAN

If you're more of a meat and potatoes kind of diner, then try **Hitching Post II**, which is also in Buellton. Known for its Western flair and generous portions, the restaurant has a reputation for its thick steaks and excellent wine. This is on the Sideways The Map tour as the where Miles' love interest Maya worked as a waitress. *Info:* www.hitchingpost2.com. Tel. 805/688-0676. Buellton. 406 E. Highway 246.

Wine Tours & Tastings

Most of the wineries along the Santa Barbara wine trails are open daily for tours and tastings. **Tastings**, which once were free, **will now run you about $10** for a few wine flights and a keepsake glass. Some vintners will apply the tasting fee towards wines purchased. Most of the wineries also have gift shops and picnic areas.

From Buellton, hop on the 101 Freeway heading south back towards Santa Barbara. The drive is about 40 minutes long. Take it easy this evening enjoying your new wine purchase or strolling along Stearns Wharf.

Sunday
After breakfast, head down to **Cabrillo Avenue** along the waterfront for the weekly **Arts & Crafts Show** held every Sunday since 1965. From 10am until dusk, local artists offer their wares for sale. You'll find everything from landmark paintings and sculptures to handcrafted wind chimes. Many artists are set up to accept major credit cards.

Once you've finished looking for a keepsake to bring home, get in the car and head to the **Santa Barbara Zoo**, which is one of my all-time favorite zoos. Located on 30 acres of botanical gardens, the zoo sits atop a knoll overlooking the ocean and estuary. You'll find more than 500 wild animals living in their natural habitats, and you'll have plenty of time to see each and every one. The most interesting resident at the zoo is the **Baringo Giraffe** who sports an extremely crooked neck. The elephants and gorilla exhibits are also among my favorite. Kids will enjoy the miniature train that encircles the park, as

ALTERNATIVE PLAN
Skip the zoo and make the **Santa Barbara Museum of Art** your Sunday afternoon destination. The museum has an impressive collection of 19th-century French art and also hosts some fascinating exhibits. Best of all, the museum is **free on Sunday**. Don't miss a chance to browse in the museum store, also located on State Street. *Info:* www.sbmuseart.org. Tel. 805/963-4364. Downtown. 1130 State Street. Open Tuesday-Sunday 11am-5pm.

well as the zoo's playground and carousel. Outside food and drink are permitted and can be enjoyed in any of the zoo's designated picnic areas. *Info:* www.santabarbarazoo.com. Tel. 805/962-5339. Beach Area. 500 Ninos Drive. Open daily 10am-5pm. Admission adults $10, $8 children.

From here, continue along Cabrillo Boulevard towards **Montecito**, which is actually part of Santa Barbara proper. Cabrillo Boulevard becomes Coast Village Road after the freeway underpass. Continue down **Coast Village Road**, park your car, and walk around Montecito. There are shops, restaurants and galleries along both sides of the street. Chances are you might rub elbows with a celebrity resident as many famous names have homes here, including Steve Martin, Rob Lowe, Kevin Costner, Kathy Ireland and Oprah Winfrey, just to name a few. Have dinner at the **Montecito Inn**, located at the corner of Olive Mill Road. The inn, built in 1928 by silent screen star Charlie Chaplin, has a charming restaurant frequented by many locals. If you want something a bit more casual, the hotel's **Montecito Café Bar** features an appetizer menu, cocktails and fine, local wines. *Info:* www.montecitoinn.com. Tel. 805/969-7894. Montecito. 1295 Coast Village Road.

From here, you can catch the 101 Freeway at Olive Mill Road and head to your next destination.

A WONDERFUL WEEK IN SANTA BARBARA

After a week in Santa Barbara you'll leave feeling like a local, knowing all the "in" spots, and probably encountering familiar faces from day to day along State Street. You'll have a chance to explore the various neighborhoods, head to the wine country and its tasting rooms, and visit some unique attractions that will be well worth your time.

RECOMMENDED PLAN: Spend two days just hanging out along State Street and the waterfront with a day to spend at the beach. You'll want another day or two to explore Santa Barbara's **Wine Country**, including the Danish town of **Solvang**. With seven days to spend along the American Riviera, you can also factor in at least one day trip – two if you're feeling adventurous. I recommend heading south to **Ventura** and then up to **Ojai** one day, and allowing another day to motor up the Central Coast to explore **Hearst Castle**.

Downtown Santa Barbara

If you stay in town you'll likely be doing a lot of walking along **State Street**. From Sola Street all the way down to the waterfront is block after block of shops, restaurants and galleries. The **Red Tile Walking Tour** *(see One Great Day in this chapter)* is a perfect way to get acquainted with downtown and, at the same time, gain an appreciation for its architecture and history.

The best way to experience downtown is on foot. But if you're not up for walking, hop aboard the **State Street Shuttle**, an electric open-air minibus that stops approximately every 10 minutes at almost every block. Look for the blue signs for pick up and drop off locations. The waterfront also has an electric shuttle that operates less frequently, about every 30 minutes, from the harbor area to the Santa Barbara Zoo with frequent stops in between. The fare for both shuttles is 25 cents a ride (exact change required).

At 1130 State Street is the **Santa Barbara Museum of Art** featuring a permanent collection of 19th century works by French artists Monet, Matisse, Degas and Chagall. There is a gift shop, café and children's gallery on the premises. Around the corner at 7 East Anapamu is the small and intriguing gallery of **Sullivan Goss**, featuring works by contemporary artists. In the gallery's rear and intimate courtyard is the **Arts & Letters Café,** a charming culinary hideaway for lunch. *Info:* www.sullivangross.com. Tel. 805/730-1463. Downtown.

State Street will eventually end its path at the foot of Stearns Wharf on Cabrillo Boulevard. This is where the Waterfront District begins. At the end of Stearns Wharf is the **Ty Warner Sea Center** (particularly good for kids) and **Santa Barbara Marine**

Center, both of which offer a glimpse into the world below the water's surface.

At the foot of Stearns Wharf is the **Bicentennial Friendship Fountain**, more commonly known as the Dolphin Fountain due to its design. In 1982 local artist Bud Bottoms sculpted the fountain in honor of Santa Barbara's 200th birthday. Dolphins were chosen as the fountain's centerpiece because the native Chumash Indians believed the aquatic mammal signified good luck.

In and around town are some enjoyable botanical attractions, including the **Santa Barbara Botanic Garden**. Located on 65 acres in the foothills, the garden was California's very first botanic garden solely dedicated to the native flora. Established in 1926, there are now more than 1,000 species of rare and indigenous plants. Be sure to wear comfortable shoes and clothes so that you can enjoy a hike through the meadows and canyons, the Redwood Forest, and stroll across the Mission Dam. Take a docent-led tour, conducted daily at 2pm and on weekends at 11am, or got it alone with a self-guided theme tour. *Info:* www.sbbg.org. Tel. 805/682-4726. Santa Barbara. 1212 Mission Canyon Road. Open daily 10am-5pm. Admission adults $8, children $6.

Best Family Fun

- The **Santa Barbara Zoo**, Tel. 805/963-5339, 500 Ninos Drive
- **Santa Barbara Museum of Natural History**, Tel. 805/682-4711, 2558 Puesta del Sol Rd.
- **Kid's World** at Alameda Park at the corner of Micheltorena and Garden Streets
- **Ostrich Land** in Solvang, Tel. 805/686-9696, 610 E. Highway 246
- **The Carousel** at Chase Palm Park on Cabrillo Boulevard near Garden Street
- Riding a **Surrey Cycle** along the beach – rentals available at the corner of State Street and Cabrillo Boulevard
- **Ty Warner Sea Center** on Stearns Wharf

The **Mission Rose Park** on Laguna Street, across from the Mission Santa Barbara, features more than 1,000 roses. Artists often capture the mission's beauty from this location, and it's an enjoyable place to visit on its own or in conjunction with a trip to the Mission.

The **Andrew Clark Bird Refuge**, located along the lagoon near the Santa Barbara Zoo, is home to a variety of birds as well as

families of ducks. If you rent a Surrey Cycle in town, you can pedal along the pathway from the pier all the way down to the refuge – about 2 miles. *Info:* 1400 E. Cabrillo Boulevard. Free.

North of Santa Barbara
As you head north, pull off Highway 101 at the Patterson exit and head towards the ocean for a couple of miles. At the end is Orchid Drive, which leads to the **Santa Barbara Orchid Estate** at 1250 Orchid Drive. Take a few minutes to enjoy one of the world's foremost collections of orchid species and hybrids. The estate, established in 1957, sits on five coastal acres and is open to the public Monday-Saturday 8am-4:30pm and on Sunday 11am-4pm. Not only can you admire, you can also purchase a plant to take home. *Info:* www.sborchid.com. Tel. 805/967-1284. Free.

Goleta
Goleta is a small, college town where the University of California, Santa Barbara, and some 18,000 co-eds are found. Aside from four golf courses, you'll also find the **South Coast Railroad Museum**, housed in an historic depot dating back to 1901. Inside is a collection of railroad artifacts, photographs and exhibits including a 300-square-foot model of a railroad. Kids will enjoy a ride on the miniature train. *Info:* www.goletadepot.com. Tel. 805/964-3540. Goleta. 300 North Los Carneros Road. Open Wednesday-Sunday 1-4pm. Free – donations accepted.

Santa Barbara's Wine Country, which I covered in this chapter under *A Fantastic Weekend*, is also north of town. Highways 154

ALTERNATIVE PLAN

Walk the campus of **UC Santa Barbara**, where of one the campus dormitories offers its residents rooms overlooking the water. The **University Art Museum**, featuring a distinguished fine art collection with more than 8,500 works and some 750,000 architectural drawings, historic photographs, writings, scrapbooks and three-dimensional objects in the Architecture and Design Collection, is free to the public. *Info:* Park in Lot 23 on campus. Nominal parking fee required. Open Wednesday-Sunday 12-5pm.

and 246, which meander through the hamlets of Los Olivos, Santa Ynez, Buellton, Ballard, and Solvang, will guide you to the wine trails and tasting rooms. If you take Highway 154 from Santa Barbara, make a point to have lunch or dinner at the historic **Cold Spring Tavern** just off the highway at 5995 Stage Coach Road. Established in 1865, this romantic retreat is a former stagecoach stop and has operated as a restaurant since 1941. If you're heading to the Wine Country on Sunday, then Cold Spring Tavern is a "must stop" for breakfast. *Info:* www.coldspringtavern.com. Tel. 805/967-0066.

If you're serious about winetasting, then let someone else do the driving. Listed below are some companies that offer everything from champagne limousine tours to open-air jeep safaris:
- **Wine 'Edventures**, www.welovewines.com. Tel. 805/965-9463
- **Santa Barbara Adventure Company**, www.sbadventureco.com. Tel. 805/773-3239

- **Cloud Climber Jeeps**, www.ccjeeps.com. Tel. 805/965-6654
- **Limousine Link**, www.santabarbaralimousinelink.com. Tel. 805/564-6654

Farmers' Markets

Want to get a taste of some local flavor, both in terms of people and culinary offerings? Then visit one of the **Farmers' Markets**, held every day of the week at a different location. Sample fresh organic fruit, listen to live music and meet the farmers themselves. My favorite is the Saturday market in downtown, at the corner of Santa Barbara & Cota Streets, 8:30am-12:30pm. *Info:* www.sbfarmersmarket.org. Tel. 805/962-5354.

South of Santa Barbara
To the south of Santa Barbara is **Summerland**, founded in 1889 as a spiritualist retreat, it was to be the "Western Whitehouse" during the Clinton administration, but for some reason that never materialized. Highway 101 cuts a swathe between the town and the shoreline. A single road that parallels the freeway is brimming with galleries, antique shops and unassuming cafes.

Further down Highway 101 is **Carpinteria**, where avocado farms and greenhouses filled with Gerbera daisies dot the hills of this agricultural beach town. Carpinteria State Beach Park, dubbed the "World's Safest Beach," is a fun place to spend the afternoon, though the temperatures rarely get above 70 degrees. **Downtown Carpinteria** is filled with shops, galleries and restaurants. During the summer the **Santa Barbara Polo and Racquet Club**, which, despite its name, is located in Carpinteria, opens up its gracious gates every Sunday to the public for its weekly polo matches. Admission is $10 per person from May to September. *Info:* www.sbpolo.com. Tel. 805/684-6683. Off Highway 101 at the Padero Lane exit.

Ventura & Ojai
About 30 minutes south of Santa Barbara is San Buenaventura, a name that has been shortened to **Ventura** over the years. Where Santa Barbara to the north is laden with famous citizens and plenty of wealth, Ventura is more of a blue-collar beach town. In recent years, however, downtown Ventura has enjoyed a renaissance with a number of new shops and restaurants occupying

once-empty storefronts. Ventura also has pristine beach conditions, which makes it popular with early-morning surfers.

Spend your time along **Main Street**, between Ventura and Chestnut Avenues in historic downtown Ventura, where there is a bulk of antique shops and restaurants. At 211 East Main Sreet is the **San Buenaventura Mission**, the 21st and final mission founded by Father Junipero Serra. Erected in 1782, this mission has wooden bells in its belfry, which calls modern-day worshipers to service. You're welcome to stroll the grounds, visit the gift shop, and enter the sanctuary. Open daily from 10am-5pm. Suggested donation is $1 per person.

From Ventura, you can take Highway 33 up to **Ojai** (pronounced Oh-hi). Highway 33 becomes West Ojai Avenue, the town's main thoroughfare, and is  approximately 30 minutes from downtown Ventura. Ojai is easily manageable by foot, but the Ojai Trolley Service does provide transportation in and around town for just a quarter. In recent years Ojai has gained a reputation as a haven for spiritual gurus, and you will see many shops and galleries specializing in crystals and other metaphysical items. Ojai is also a **fledgling artists' colony** with a fleet of galleries, and you'll also find a web of trails for hiking and horseback riding.

Downtown Ojai is home to the Mission Revival-style **Arcade**, erected in 1917 by Ohio glass magnate Edmund D. Libbey. It is the focal point of town and is where a bulk of shops, galleries and boutiques are located. Consider having afternoon tea at **Tottingham Court**, 242 East Ojai Avenue, a unique store that carries a treasure trove of items. If you're a bibliophile, visit the landmark **Bart's Books**, an outdoor bookstore at 302 West Matilija Street that carries shelves and shelves of used books. You could literally spend hours here looking for hard-to-find titles.

A day in Ojai is all about enjoying the outdoors. **Libbey Park,** located across from the Arcade, is a great place to bring the kids to play. The **Ojai Valley Trail** can be picked up in town at Fox Road, and is open from dawn to dusk. *Info:* Tel. 805/654-3951 for recorded information.

About 20 miles away is the small community of **Fillmore** where you'll find the **Fillmore & Western Railway Company.** When these classic Pullman sleepers and vintage parlor cars are not being summoned on some movie set, they are ferrying passengers around the valley. Some of the onboard events you could take part in include wine train excursions, murder mystery dinners, and barbecue outings. *Info:* www.fwry.com. Tel. 805/524-2546.

For lunch or dinner you can dine elegantly or extremely casual. I recommend dining at one of the three restaurants located at the **Ojai Valley Inn & Spa.** All venues have outdoor terraces that are just breathtaking, and the service and food are superb. Another suggestion is **The Ranch House**, a favorite of Paul Newman's and an elegant outdoor setting complete with trickling stream and romantic, candlelit tables. *Info:* www.theranchhouse.com. Tel. 805/646-2360. 500 South Lomita Avenue. On the other end of the spectrum is the **Oak Pit** in nearby Oak View, which you passed on your way to Ojai. This roadhouse shack serves the most delicious tri-tip barbecue, coleslaw and corn on the cob. It's nothing fancy, just good food. *Info:* Tel. 805/649-9903. 820 N. Ventura Avenue at Highway 33.

Hearst Castle
Located about 150 miles from Santa Barbara in San Simeon, **Hearst Castle** is one of the largest historic house museums in the United States. Designed by famed architect Julia Morgan for newspaper mogul William Randolph Hearst, the "little home" that Hearst envisioned ended up being an extravagant—at least by most people's standards—165-room mansion with a 127 acres of gardens, terraces, pools and walkways. After Hearst's death, the estate was donated to the People of the State of California in 1957. Today the California State Parks Department does an incredible job at keeping the estate looking like a private resi-

dence. There are five tours available with each one lasting approximately two hours; a little longer if you include the five-mile bus trip up the hill. You will likely only have time for one tour, maybe two, and advanced reservations are required.

Tour 1 is recommended for first-time visitors and takes you to some of the gardens, through the 18-room guesthouse, the Neptune and Roman pools, and the main house. **Tour 2** will give you a closer look at the main home's upper floors, Hearst's private suite, the libraries and the kitchen. **Tours 3 & 4** take you to additional gardens, residential quarters, the wine cellar, and terraces. **Tour 5** is a special tour that allows you to see the castle at night. Each tour, which is subject to change due to renovation conditions, reveals architectural gems and numerous works of priceless art. *Info:* www.hearstcastle.com. Reservations required: 800/444-4445. San Simeon. Tours 1-4 are offered several times daily from 8:40am-4:40pm; Tour 5 is a seasonal tour offered

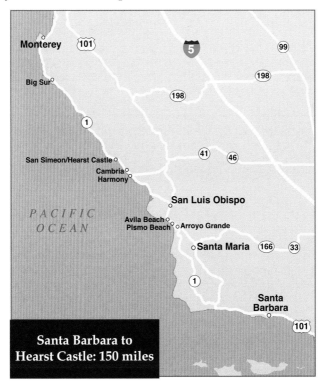

March-May and September-December from 6:30-8:10pm. To reach Hearst Castle take Highway 101 north to San Luis Obispo, then Highway 1 north for approximately 40 miles. The one-way trip is about three hours from Santa Barbara.

It's a three-hour drive each way to and from Hearst Castle. Swap a night in Santa Barbara for a night along the Central Coast. The closest accommodations are a string of motels along Highway 1 in San Simeon.

7. PALM SPRINGS

Palm Springs is a desert oasis for Southern Californians; a place to head for the weekend and soak up the sun. Palm Springs is actually part of the **Coachella Valley** and the desert resort communities, which feature several other key destinations, including Cathedral City, Desert Hot Springs, Indian Wells, Indio, La Quinta, Palm Desert and Rancho Mirage.

The best time of year to visit the desert resort communities is during the late fall through early spring when the average temperature hovers around 70 degrees. Most people make the exodus to Palm Springs to relax by the pool, play a round or two of golf, hit the tennis court, and book some much-needed spa treatments. The area is also very gay-friendly, and there is an active gay social life here. There are some unique attractions as well as some lovely places to enjoy an early morning hike. In Palm Springs and the surrounding area you can really do as much or as little as you please without feeling like you've missed out on anything.

ONE GREAT DAY IN PALM SPRINGS

Most people heading to the Palm Springs area, maybe yourself included, have designs of sitting by the pool or heading to the golf course. A spa treatment might also top the list. But if you want to quench your thirst for the desert and its unique offerings in just a day, you'll have enough time to visit **The Living Desert**, stroll along **Palm Canyon Drive** peering into shops and galleries, and slurp down a famous **date shake** at a 95-year-old date farm.

Begin your day with breakfast — New York-style — at **Manhattan in the Desert** in downtown Palm Springs. The restaurant opens daily at 7am and offers a full range of breakfast options including a classic plate of smoked salmon, tomatoes, onions, capers, cream cheese and a fist-sized bagel. *Info:* 2665 E. Palm Canyon Drive.

After breakfast, visit the **Palm Springs Walk of Stars** located in the heart of Palm Springs along Palm Canyon Drive. The concept is similar to that of the Hollywood Walk of Fame and honors celebrities who have lived or frequented the area since the 1920s. Tributes are also paid to the local pioneers who helped establish the community. Familiar names include Elizabeth Taylor, Elvis Presley, Frank Sinatra and former mayor and congressman Sonny Bono.

By now, the stores along **Palm Canyon Drive** should be open. This is the heart of Palm Springs where you'll find block after block of shops, restaurants and galleries. At night the soaring palm trees that line the road are draped in tiny, white lights. Most of the shops are independent retailers, but there are some national stores along here as well.

Next, you'll want to head out to Palm Desert and El Paseo. Tucked discreetly behind Highway 111 is the **Gardens on El Paseo** shopping complex, which has earned a reputation as the "Rodeo Drive of the Desert" because of its fine shops, restaurants

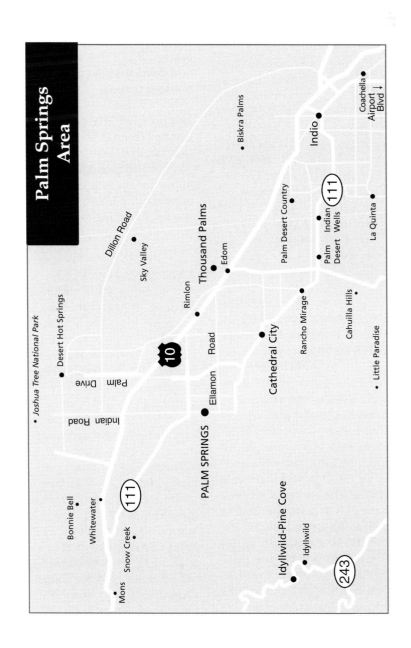

Palm Springs Area

Joshua Tree National Park
Desert Hot Springs
Dillon Road
Sky Valley
Biskra Palms
Indio
Coachella
Airport Blvd
111
Palm Desert Country
Indian Wells
La Quinta
Palm Desert
Thousand Palms
Edom
Rimlon
Rancho Mirage
Cahuilla Hills
Little Paradise
10
Ellamon Road
Cathedral City
Palm Drive
Indian Road
PALM SPRINGS
Bonnie Bell
Whitewater
111
Snow Creek
Mons
Idyllwild-Pine Cove
Idyllwild
243

Villagefest

If you happen to be visiting Palm Springs on a Thursday evening, you're in luck. Several blocks of Palm Canyon Drive are closed to vehicular traffic as **Villagefest**, a weekly arts and crafts gathering with nearly 200 vendors plus entertainment, gets underway. The nearby **Palm Springs Art Museum** offers free admission on this night as well.

horn sheep, Oryx, giraffes, zebras, cheetahs and meerkats. Within the park is **Village WaTuTu**, an authentic replica of a village found in northeast Africa replete with mud-walled huts crowned with grass-thatched roofs. Master storytellers weave tales of African and Native American folklore, and the village is home to creatures native to Africa. The Living Desert also has a play area for children, as well as docent-led tours of the facility's animal hospital where, from behind a glass partition, you're allowed to observe medical procedures and examinations that are taking place in the small and large animal treatment rooms. The

and galleries. There are only a few key blocks to cover. Have lunch at **Cuistot** (*see Palm Springs Best Eats*), a creative and delicious restaurant with outdoor seating.

Not far from El Paseo is **The Living Desert**, a zoo-like destination that sits on an 1,200 acres of arid desert land and is home to approximately 400 animals and more than 130 species, including coyotes, big-

ALTERNATIVE PLAN

If you enjoy mid-century modern architecture and you're an Elvis Presley fan, have I got a place for you. Dubbed the **Elvis Honeymoon Hideaway**, because the King leased the house in 1966 and spent his 1967 honeymoon to Priscilla under this very roof, is now open for tours by arrangement only. Call in advance for an up close and personal look at this desert-style Graceland. *Info:* Tel. 800/347-7746. Afterwards, dine at **Copley's on Palm Canyon** housed in an enchanting Spanish cottage once owned by actor **Cary Grant**. *Info:* Tel. 760/327-9555. Palm Springs. 621 N. Palm Canyon Drive.

Living Desert also has a garden featuring many plants
indigenous to the area. *Info:*
www.livingdesert.org. Tel.
760/346-5694. Palm Desert.
47-900 Portola Avenue.
Open daily September 1-
June 15 from 9am-5pm,
closed summers. Admission
adults $11.95, children $7.50.

By now you may be feeling parched from the desert heat. If you
didn't know it, you are in the "Date Capital of the World," a
reference to the fruit grown here, not the singles scene. So you
can't visit the Coachella Valley without having a signature date
shake. Head to the **Oasis Date Gardens** in Indian Wells, a 175-
acre working date ranch, that whips up a mean date shake. Enjoy
your fruity concoction at a table near the country-style store,
where you can pick up dates and olives to bring home; or take it
along on the free ranch tours offered at 10:30am and 2:30pm. *Info:*
www.oasisdategardens.com. Tel.760/399-5665. Indian Wells. 59-
111 Highway 111.

On your way out of town, grab one last desert dinner along Palm
Canyon Drive in Palm Springs. If your timeline is tight and you
don't time for dinner, grab a
date shake on your way out of
the area at **Hadley Fruit Orchards** in Cabazon, just off
Interstate 10 heading west towards Los Angeles and Or-
ange County.

Shopper Hopper

If you're spending the night
at a Palm Desert property,
take advantage of the **Shopper Hopper**. This convenient
shuttle service makes a continuous loop through Palm
Desert's main shopping districts, attractions and hotels.
Enjoy an air-conditioned ride
for free. *Info:* www.palm-
desert.org. Tel. 760/342-3451.

A FANTASTIC PALM SPRINGS AREA WEEKEND

Nothing beats a weekend in Palm Springs – just ask your fellow pool loungers, many of whom make the pilgrimage from LA, San Diego and Orange County on a regular basis. There is something very relaxing about spending a few days in the desert. Time ticks at a slower pace, attractions are few and far between, and nothing beats those warm, Arabian-style nights.

Friday Night
If it's just you and your significant other, I highly recommend you spoil yourselves with a stay at the **Willows Historic Palm Springs Inn** *(see Palm Springs Best Sleeps)*. You won't regret it. If, on the other hand, you've got your hands full of luggage and kids, then check into one of the larger, full-service resorts *(see Palm Springs Best Sleeps)*. Grab a casual meal and an outdoor table at **Las Casuelas Terraza** *(see Palm Springs Best Eats)* along Palm Canyon Drive. Sip the restaurant's signature and salt-rimmed margaritas while enjoying live entertainment.

Saturday
Begin your day early before the sun begins to heat up. Grab breakfast at the hotel to save time, then make the first stop of the day with a trip to the top of Mt. San Jacinto via the **Palm Springs Aerial Tramway** (off Highway 111 at Tramway Road in Palm Springs). The tramway was conceived in the 1930s, but wasn't

 completed until 1953. Two 80-passenger gondolas, which feature revolving floors to offer 360-degree views en route, ferry passengers up the steep incline while passing through five climate zones, from the Sonoran desert to the

alpine wilderness, before reaching the top of **Mt. San Jacinto**. Once at the top you can take a short hike through the fir forest of **Mt. San Jacinto Wilderness State Park**, hang out in the hilltop restaurant warming yourself with a cup of hot java or, weather permitting, play in the snow. Keep in mind that it's typically 40 degrees cooler at the top—remember, you've traveled 8,516 feet from the desert floor—so be sure to tuck a hat, glove and scarf in your coat pocket. *Info:* The first tramcar begins its ascent at 10am Monday-Friday, at 8am on weekends and the last car makes its way down the mountain at 9:45pm. Round-trip tram tickets are $21.95 adults, $14.95 children.

Top of the World Eats!

You can spend an hour at the top of the mountain or the entire day, it just depends on your interests. Plan to have lunch at the "top of the world" at one of the mountain's two restaurants. **Peaks** offers a more upscale experience with a menu of contemporary California cuisine with an emphasis on seafood and pasta, while the **Pines Café** offers both a casual ambiance and menu. Both restaurants offer great views. If neither lunch nor dinner is on the agenda, then enjoy a cocktail at **The Lookout Lounge** nearby. *Info:* Tel. 760/325-4537 to make reservations or book the Ride 'n' Dinner combination ticket.

Not one for mile-high adventures? Then stay grounded on the desert floor and take a **self-driven Architecture Drive** through Palm Springs. Famous for its classic, mid-century architecture, Palm Springs is like a museum without walls. Nearly every block has some building or home designed by the likes of Richard Neutra, Donald Wexler or Albert Frey. A map listing a tremendous variety of these amazing modern sites, including the Frey-designed Tramway Gas Station at 2901 North Palm Canyon Drive, is produced by the Palm Springs Modern Committee. The full-color foldout map includes the structure's name, address, architect, and the year it was built, coupled with several stunning photographs and short profiles of the best-known local architects. *Info:* www.psmodcom.com. Maps are $8, and can be purchased via mail at Palm Springs Modern Maps, PO Box 4738, Palm Springs, CA 92263.

Wind down in the afternoon with a classic mud bath the famed **Two Bunch Palms** in Desert Hot Springs. The resort, whose thick  mud is actually a million-year-old, mineral-enriched, green clay mixture, has a day spa where treatments can be booked up to a month in advance. Book the Egyptian Wrap where you get a dry brushing before being wrapped in a warm coat of clay, bundled in a blanket like a burrito and finished off with a oil massage. Or just request a private mud bath in the sun. *Info:* www.twobunchpalms.com. Tel. 760/329-8791. Desert Hot Springs. 67425 Two Bunch Palms Trail.

End the day with an elegant evening at **Le Vallauris**. This will be especially convenient if your staying at The Willows Historic Palm Springs Inn as it's located across the street. The tuxedoed sommelier can suggest the perfect wine for your meal, and the owner will likely pay a visit to your table as he makes the rounds through the intimate restaurant. Book a table on the terrace and enjoy the desert sky at night. Afterwards, stroll along **Palm Canyon Drive** before turning in for the night.

Sunday
Start with a quick breakfast at **More than a Mouthful** (134 Tahquitz Canyon Way), a tiny sidewalk café with good, cheap food and a local flavor. After breakfast head to the **Palm Springs Air Museum,**

ALTERNATIVE PLAN
Experience some vintage as well as some new Palm Springs in the same day! Stop into **Melvyn's** (200 West Ramon Road) at the Ingleside Inn, a haunt of Frank Sinatra's. Order a classic martini before heading off to **Falls Steakhouse and Martini Bar** (155 South Palm Canyon Drive) where a younger crowd gravitates. Both restaurants offer great dining experiences, one old school and the other unconventional.

where one of the largest collection of World War II propeller-driven planes is housed in a pair of air-conditioned buildings. The static display of vintage aircraft have been meticulously maintained and are in flying condition. There is also an ex-

cellent display of vintage photographs and memorabilia chronicling the history of aviation during the war. *Info:* www.palmspringsairmuseum.org. Tel. 760/778-6262. Palm Springs. 745 North Gene Autry Trail. Open daily 10am-5pm. Admission adults $10, $8.50 children.

The afternoon should be spent at the **Village Green Heritage Center**. The complex is home to a pair of original 19th-century homes. The 1885 McCallum Adobe, home to one of the area's earliest settlers, contains personal artifacts, including Indian ware. Miss Cornelia White's House was built from railroad ties in 1894 and displays much of the owner's possessions, such as the family bible, the first telephone in Palm Springs, and paintings by Carl Eytel.

ALTERNATIVE PLAN
If you prefer art to aviation, then head to the **Palm Springs Art Museum**, established in 1938, the museum is the center of the desert art community. There is a large permanent collection of Modern and Contemporary American works by renowned artists, as well as special exhibits and architectural holdings. Be sure to visit the Sculpture Garden and the museum store. *Info:* www.psmuseum.org. Tel. 760/325-7186. Palm Springs. 101 Museum Drive. Open Tuesday-Saturday 10am-5pm, until 8pm on Thursday for Villagefest (free admission). Admission $12.50 adults, $5 children.

Info: www.palmspringshistoricalsociety.com. Tel. 760/323-8297. Palm Springs. 221-223 South Palm Canyon Drive. Open October-May 10m-3pm. Admission $1.

Want someone else to do the driving and guide you around while in Palm Springs? Check out these unique tour companies:
• **Canyon Jeep Tours**, Tel. 760/320-4600, offering nature tours to Indian Canyon or Joshua Tree
• **Desert Adventures**, Tel. 760/324-JEEP, also offering tours to Indian Canyon or Joshua Tree
• **Celebrity Tours of Palm Springs**, Tel. 760/770-2700, narrated driving tours of the stars' homes
• **Covered Wagon Tours, Inc.**, Tel. 760/347-2161, unique covered wagon tours of the desert complete with a barbecue dinner feast and country music.

If your evening plans call for a freeway ride back to Los Angeles or Orange County, make a point to stop by the **Mission Inn** in Riverside. If you have a night to spare, you might even want to stay here on Sunday and drive the rest of the way back the following day. The hotel dates back to 1876 and is one of Southern California's best-kept secrets. Richard and Pat Nixon were married here, and Ronald and Nancy Reagan spent part of their honeymoon here as well. The four-winged property looks like something straight out of Europe, and I highly recommend you take the 70-minute guided historic tour. Have dinner at one of the hotel's highly acclaimed restaurants before getting back on the road or retiring for the night in one of the inn's guest rooms. *Info:* www.missioninn.com. Tel. 951/784-0300. Downtown Riverside. 3649 Mission Inn Avenue.

A WONDERFUL WEEK IN THE PALM SPRINGS AREA

With an entire week to spend in the desert, you'll have more than enough time to experience some of the key attractions and still be a regular at the swimming pool or hotel spa. Use the morning hours to do your exploring, then return to your resort in the afternoon for a little rest and relaxation.

RECOMMENDED PLAN: The key to visiting Palm Springs is that you'll want to pace yourself because the whole idea of coming to the desert is to relax and rejuvenate. Use a couple of mornings to enjoy the landscape with a hike through **Indian Canyons**, a ride up to **Mt. San Juancinto** via the Palm Springs Aerial Tramway, or take in a horseback ride at **Smoke Tree Stables**. Then set aside a day to visit either **Pioneer Town** or **Joshua Tree**, depending on your interests. You'll also want to take some time for a spa treatment, reserve a tee time on one of the golf courses, and visit one of the nearby casinos in the evening.

Palm Springs has a few hidden gems that most visitors don't get to experience. **Indian Canyons** is one of them. Made up of four majestic gorges filled with jutting cliffs, leafy palm trees, natural pools and gushing waterfalls, this gift from Mother Nature will take a bit of effort on your part to reach but, if you're a nature lover, it's well worth it.

Only three of the four canyons are accessible to visitors. **Andreas Canyon** is a breathtaking ravine with traces of primitive Indian life includ-

Don't Miss ...

- The **Palm Springs Aerial Tramway**
- Exploring **Indian Canyons**
- A classic **Date Shake** at Oasis Date Gardens
- A self-driving **Mid-Century Architectural Tour**
- The **Fabulous Palm Springs Follies**
- A mud math at **Two Bunch Palms**
- Gambling at an **Indian Casino**
- A desert **horseback ride** at Smoke Tree Ranch

ing rock etchings and indentations as a result of indigenous women crushing beans and nuts against the hard surfaces for centuries. Nearby **Murray Canyon** is home to the Seven Sisters, a fleet of natural pools connected by cascading waterfalls. Natural rock formations, some boasting 20-foot drops, will provide you with natural platforms for plunging into the cool waters. **Palm Canyon**, which stretches some 15 miles, completes the canyon trio. Known for its 3,000 verdant palms—some as old as 2,000 years—you will discover more natural pools inside this canyon.

Indian Canyons has a trading post, picnic grounds, lots of hiking trails that run along streams and horse trails. This could easily take an entire day. *Info:* Tel. 800/790-3398. From Palm Springs head south on Palm Canyon Drive towards Indian Canyons – it's about five miles from the center of town. Open daily 8am-5pm. Admission $8.

Another best-kept secret is the **Palms to Pines scenic drive**. Enjoy a 130-mile scenic route traversing the desert's forest (note: this is not a misprint!) and alpine roads. You'll find the terrain to be extremely diverse, and be on the lookout for deer, an abundant of birds, and even herds of bighorn sheep. Along Highway 74 you'll pass **Lake Hemet**, a municipal reservoir that attracts wintering waterfowl. As you motor along Highway 243 pull over to the Indian Vista overlook. Take a few moments to enjoy the oak trees and local residents, including mule deer, acorn woodpeckers, alligator lizards and more. *Info:* From Palm Desert, follow Highway 74 to the fork branching off to the right, head towards Idyllwild and Mountain Center, continue into the

Must-Try Spa Treatments

- **Green Tea Ginger Enzyme Wrap** at the Estrella Spa at the Viceroy Hotel
- **Blackberry Hand Treatment** at the Agua Serena Spa at Hyatt Grand Champions Resort
- **Pittura Festa Mud Painting Massage** at the Well Spa at the Miramonte Resort & Spa
- **Cahuilla Sage Wrap** at La Quinta Resort & Club
- **Caviar Facial** at the Renaissance Esmeralda Resort & Spa

the San Gorgonio Pass and through Banning. Return via Highway 243 to Interstate 10 to Highway 111.

If you're visiting the area from November to May, it's almost required that you take in an evening at **The Fabulous Palm Springs Follies**. The folly clan takes you back to the days of vaudeville with song and dance extravaganzas from the '20s, '30s and '40s. The performers, ages 54-to-86, are young at heart and more energetic than entertainers half their ages. Many of the cast members were Hollywood contract players back in the day and really know a thing or two about entertaining. The show varies from year to year, but you can expect your money's worth. *Info:* www.psfollies.com. Tel. 760/327-0255. Palm Springs. The Plaza Theatre. 128 S. Palm Canyon Drive.

Joshua Tree & Environs

While you may think all deserts are created equal, a trip to **Joshua Tree National Park** may have you thinking otherwise. The park joins together Southern California's high and low deserts to create nearly 800,000 acres of barren land. Located about 50 miles from Palm Springs, you should allow for at least a half day at Joshua Tree.

The lower elevated **Colorado Desert**, at a mere 3,000 feet, occupies the eastern half of the park and is dominated by creosote bush. Its arid climate is the ideal environment for harvesting the spiny ocotillo and cholla cactus. The higher, moister **Mojave Desert** is where the Joshua Tree thrives along the western half of the park. Clusters of fan palm oasis dot the grounds where the presence of water naturally occurs at or near the surface, which is the only reason these trees are able to survive.

Twisted and cragged rock help to form the rugged mountains, while granite monoliths assist in creating the desert mosaic.

One of the early inhabitants of this region was the **Pinto Man**, who hunted and gathered along a slow moving river, which gorged the terrain that eventually became the parched Pinto Basin. Native American later roamed the region harvesting pinyon nuts, mesquite beans, acorns and cactus fruit, leaving their mark with petroglyphs and other impressions of their existence. The late 1800s saw a influx of explorers, cattlemen and miners in search of gold. In the 1930s, homesteaders from various parts of the country arrived in search of free land.

Quail Mountain, at 5,814 above sea level, is the park's highest point of elevation; Pinto Basin earns the lowest point of elevation at 1,200 feet. Aside from the two desert basins, Joshua Tree is also home to a half-dozen mountain ranges. *Info:* Tel. 760/367-5500. Take Interstate 10 east to Twentynine Palms Highway to Route 62 north to Twentynine Palms. Turn right on National Park Drive and travel for a half-mile until you reach the Oasis Visitor Center. Stop by to get additional information, including current park conditions. The center is open year-round from 8am-5pm and there are restrooms, phones, a bookstore, beverages and picnic tables.

On your way to Joshua Tree you may want to make a side trip to **Pioneer Town**. Actors Gene Autry and Roy Rogers built this Old West relic in the 1940s for the purpose of filming movies. The two made some use of their fabricated city before it eventually

Joshua Tree in 240 Minutes

- Begin your tour at the **visitor center**
- Limit your time to the **main park roads**, you'll cover more ground
- Take a **hike** on one of 12 self-guiding nature trails
- If the skies are clear, the 20-minute drive to **Key Views** is worth every second just to see the vistas of the Salton Sea and Mexico beyond.

materialized into a modern-day ghost town. As time passed people actually began inhabiting the railroad-tie and adobe structures turning movie facades into false-front buildings that served as homes and businesses. Today this faux frontier land is an unincorporated town in the Morongo Basin region halfway between Palm Springs and Joshua Tree. You'll want to take a walk down **Mane Street**, which is private property but pedestrians are welcome. Mock gunfights are often staged, and you will really feel as if you've stepped back in time or, at least, onto a movie set. *Info:* Pioneer Town is located off Highway 62 between Palm Springs and Joshua Tree. Estimate about a 30-minute drive.

ALTERNATIVE PLAN
If you want to spend more than just a few hours at Joshua Tree, consider staying overnight at **The 29 Palms Inn**. The inn, located in Twenty-nine Palms, the gateway to Joshua Tree, has a number of freestanding bungalows and cottages starting as low as $75 per night with a continental breakfast included. Onsite pool and restaurant. *Info:* www.29palmsinn.com. Tel. 760/367-3505.

Just outside of Palm Springs on Interstate 10 in Cabazon is the **Desert Hills Premium Outlets**. If you like to shop and don't want to pay retail, then you'll enjoy the bargain hunting that takes place at this sprawling, outdoor plaza. There are more than 100 stores, including Coach, Ralph Lauren, Bebe, Calvin Klein and more. The list is never-ending.

Afterwards, head next door to the kitschy **World's Biggest Dinosaurs**. Claude K. Bell began sculpting these pair of prehistoric icons in the late 1960s, and the two, Dinny and Mr. Rex, are now desert landmarks. They've appeared in many movies, and Dinny's stomach actually houses a gift shop. While you're here, pop in to Morongo Casino, which has all the bells and whistles of a Las Vegas-style casino. The casino houses plenty of slots and table games, as well as restaurants, entertainment and even a spa. *Info:* Cabazon is located off Interstate 10. Exit at Field Road to begin at the Desert Hills Premium Outlets.

Palm Springs Golf Getaway

If your ideal Palms Springs getaway is to do nothing but golf, then contact **Palm Springs Golf Vacations**. It's one-stop shopping for golfers. The company will arrange an itinerary that will include accommodations, advance tee times, private instruction, transportation and whatever else is required to make the most of your time in the desert and on the course. *Info:* www.psgolfvacations.com. Tel. 800/774-6531.

Either to or from Cabazon you'll notice a fleet of futuristic structures built from steel. These **4,000 windmills** deliver electricity throughout the Coachella Valley and beyond. You can actually take a 90-minute eco-tour of the facility aboard an electric, windmill-charged tram where you'll get the scoop on the current utilization of wind power and be privy to some spectacular desert landscape. *Info:* www.windmilltours.com. Tel. 760/251-1997. Located at the Indian Avenue exit off Interstate 10. Call first for a reservation.

8. SOUTHERN CALIFORNIA IN TWO WEEKS

With 14 days to spend in Southern California you'll have time to visit most of the main attractions, as well as some treasures that aren't as well known. You'll also have plenty of time to relax by the pool if you chose or enjoy a spa treatment, play a few rounds of golf or take an unexpected daytrip to a dreamy destination. You won't return home feeling as if you need a *vacation from your vacation*. Instead, you'll explore the region at a leisurely pace, inhale the scenery, and take pleasure in your surroundings simply by living in the moment.

Not only will you visit the major metropolises, **Los Angeles** and **San Diego**, you'll also get to experience the beauty of the **coastline, desert** and **wine-growing regions**. You won't just be a passive visitor to Southern California; instead, you'll be a passionate participant free to experience only the best that the region has to offer.

RECOMMENDED PLAN: With LAX offering service from nearly every region of the United States, as well as internationally, this is likely the airport you'll arrive and depart from. I've created an itinerary that allows you to spend three days in Los Angeles, two days in Palm Springs, three days in San Diego, three days in Orange County and three days in Santa Barbara before returning to Los Angeles to catch your flight. I've planned it so that you'll only drive two and a half hours or less from destination to destination. Refer to maps in the previous chapters; see page 8 for a list.

Note: If you have an early morning flight to catch back home, you can always eliminate one night from your itinerary so that you can spend a night at a hotel near the airport. Both the Westin Los Angeles Airport, Tel. 310/ 216-5858, or the Best Western Suites Hotel, Tel. 310/677-7773, are located less than five minutes from the airport.

ALTERNATIVE PLAN
If your trip begins in **San Diego** because your flight terminates at this airport, then you'll motor over to Palm Springs then on to Los Angeles, up to Santa Barbara, then down to Orange County before returning to San Diego to catch your flight. You'll still have the same amount of time at each destination. If you need to catch an early flight from San Diego, eliminate one night along the way and spend your last night in downtown near the airport.

LOS ANGELES
Fast-paced and sometimes frenzied, Los Angeles is an urban oasis with many facets. It has culture and pop culture, red carpets and ruby sunsets, historic landmarks and haute destinations. LA is a force to be reckoned with, and a great place to begin your Southern California sojourn. You'll spend three days in the City of Angels, which should give you ample time to get a taste for downtown, Hollywood, Beverly Hills and Santa Monica.

Start your trip to Los Angeles at the corner of **Hollywood and Highland** where Tinseltown's past and present collide. On this very corner is the **Hollywood Roosevelt Hotel** where the very first **Academy Awards** presentation was held, as well as the **Kodak Theatre**, Oscar's *new* home. Located here as well are **Grauman's Chinese Theatre** and the **Forecourt of the Stars**, where icons past and present have left their indelible marks in cement. Take a stroll down Hollywood Boulevard and neighboring streets to admire the names along the **Hollywood Walk of Fame**, and visit the Hollywood Museum located inside the historic **Max Factor Building** (1660 N. Highland) where you'll find many exhibits and artifacts chronicling the industry's history.

Head south on Highland Avenue, then east on Santa Monica Boulevard until you reach the **Hollywood Forever Cemetery** near the corner of Van Ness to see the tombstones of the famous and infamous. At **Sunset and Gower**, just a bit northeast, is a great photo opportunity if you're interested in capturing the **Hollywood Sign** on film.

From the cemtery, turn right onto Santa Monica Boulevard and make another left on Van Ness. At Melrose Avenue, take another right. You'll pass by the famed gates of **Paramount Studios** at 5555 Melrose. Near Melrose and La Brea Avenues is **Pink's Hot Dogs** — look for the long line — where celebrity-signed photos cover nearly every inch of wall in the shack-like dining room. If time permits, grab a hot dog at this LA landmark before continuing west on Melrose Avenue. Between La Brea and Fairfax is the **Melrose Avenue shopping district** featuring a fleet of stores, restaurants andfunky finds. At Fairfax turn left and continue down to 3rd Street to the **Farmers Market**, an outdoor shopping and dining destination. You might see a celebrity picking out fruit or sampling the crepes. Next door is **The Grove**, an upscale outdoor center with beautiful landscapes, a collection of stores and outdoor dining.

From The Grove you can continue south on Fairfax Boulevard to Wilshire Boulevard in the heart of the **mid-Wilshire** district (also known as Museum Row and Miracle Mile). Within a mile and a half are the **George C. Page Museum** and **La Brea Tarpits**, the **Los Angeles County Museum of Art**, and the **Peterson Automotive Museum**. Heading west on Wilshire Boulevard, you'll begin your foray into the lifestyles of the rich and famous once you hit **Beverly Hills**. At the foot of **Rodeo Drive** is the **Regent Beverly Wilshire Hotel**, where Julia Roberts' character stayed in *Pretty Woman* and, in real life, where Warren Beatty lived for many years. To your right is the famed Rodeo Drive with its many designer shops and jewelers.

ALTERNATIVE PLAN

After leaving Farmers Market and The Grove, take a drive along the original long and winding road: **Sunset Boulevard**. You'll head north on Fairfax and hang a left on Sunset Boulevard, near the beginning of the **Sunset Strip**. The road will take you through Beverly Hills, past multi-million dollar mansions, wind past the UCLA campus and through Brentwood before arriving at the ocean in Pacific Palisades near Santa Monica.

When you reach the corner of Wilshire and Santa Monica Boulevards, you can either continue on Wilshire to Santa Monica, or turn left onto Santa Monica Boulevard, part of Route 66, and travel through Century City to reach the beach This is the less interesting route. If you continue on Wilshire Boulevard, it will take you through the **Wilshire Corridor**, where many celebrities have pied-a-terres in the luxurious high-rise buildings that line the avenue, past Westwood Village, home to the UCLA campus, onward to moneyed Brent-

wood and finally to Santa Monica. Once here, visit the famed **Santa Monica Pier** and its amusements, **Third Street Promenade** for shopping and dining and, of course, the beach. To the south of Santa Monica is **Venice Beach** and its colorful boardwalk and notorious **Muscle Beach**; to the north is Malibu, where **The Getty Villa** and **Pepperdine University** are located.

From Santa Monica, you can take the Interstate 10 Freeway to **downtown Los Angeles**. Exit 9th Street and head north to 9th and Los Angeles Streets where you'll find yourself in the heart of the **Fashion District.** This is the place to come for clothing and accessory bargains. Make sure to take a walk down Santee Alley where you can haggle for a better price on almost anything. From here, make your way north to **Olvera Street**, a Mexican-style mercado and founding point of Los Angeles with many historic structures and adobes to visit.

Cross the street to **Union Station**, built in 1939 and considered the last of America's great train depots. Grab a French dip sandwich across the street at **Philippe's, The Original**, founded in 1908 and located at the corner of Alameda and Ord. Afterwards walk up Ord and mosey around **Chinatown** and its herb shops and landmarks. Turn right on Broadway toward **Central Plaza,** where the clicking of mahjong tiles can be heard from open windows and the smell of freshly-baked goods waft down the street.

PALM SPRINGS
The ultimate resort town, Palm Springs is a popular spot for Southern Californians to flee for a weekend of rest and relaxation from late fall to early spring. You'll have time for some key attractions, as well as some much-needed hours to spend by the pool, on the golf course or getting pampered at a luxe spa.

En Route
Travel from Los Angeles to Palm Springs east on Interstate 10, where the scenery changes from urban to suburban to ruggedly rural as you leave the city behind. On your way out, you might want to take a short detour to the 60 Freeway East and then to the 91 Freeway East to the Mission Inn exit. Here you can take an hour to walk around the historic **Mission Inn** in downtown Riverside. The hotel is a magnificent mix of many architectural styles, and its storied history is uncovered on daily docent-led walking tours. Afterwards, continue

east on the 91 Freeway where you can pick up Interstate 10 East just a few miles down the road and continue your journey onward to Palm Springs.

In Town
One of the first landmarks you'll encounter on your way into Palm Springs is the **Tramway Gas Station**, the gateway to the Palm Springs Aerial Tramway. While this may not be your first stop on your two-day getaway, you'll want to consider taking the tramway to the top of Mt. San Jacinto as this is quite an experience.

Highway 111, which links the desert resort communities, becomes Palm Canyon Drive in Palm Springs. This thoroughfare is considered the hub of Palm Springs and is lined with an array of shops, restaurants, galleries and pedestrians. If you're in town on a Thursday night, be sure to make your way to Palm Canyon Drive for **Villagefest**, a weekly gathering where local artists display their works on the street. Palm Springs also has two stellar museums catering to different interests. The **Palm Springs Air Museum** will appeal to history and aircraft enthusiasts, while the **Palm Springs Art Museum** features a collection of modern and contemporary works by renowned artists.

Continuing down Highway 111, you'll drive through Cathedral City and Rancho Mirage before reaching Palm Desert and the **Gardens on El Paseo**, a chic shopping and arts district dubbed "the Beverly Hills of the desert." Nearby is **The Living Desert**, a zoo-like destination that sits on 1,200 acres of arid desert land and is home to approximately 400 animals and more than 130 species, including coyotes, bighorn sheep, Oryx, giraffes, zebras, cheetahs and meerkats.

From Palm Desert continue your trek along Highway 111 to Indian Wells and a quick visit to the **Oasis Date Garden** where you'll take a tour of a date farm and sample a thick, unforgettable date shake – a desert delicacy. Next to Indian Wells is La Quinta and its **Old Town Shopping District**, which makes for a nice outing. The historic and luxe **La Quinta Resort & Club** is also located here. If you're not staying on the property, which is steeped in history and Hollywood lore, you may want to dine at one of the restaurants on the premises or just take a quick look around.

For your second day, you'll want to experience the ultimate Palm Springs getaway. Transla-tion: play, relax and make little effort to exert yourself. Head to the golf course, check out one of the public tennis clubs or reserve court time at your desert resort, drape yourself across a mas-sage table at one of the re-sort spas, coat yourself in a  mud bath and bask under the sun, or just lounge under an umbrella by the pool and do nothing.

SAN DIEGO
With three days to spend in San Diego, you'll want to wander the **Gaslamp Quarter** and downtown harbor area, cross over to Coronado Island, do a little historic sightseeing in Old Town or Point Loma, make time for one of the theme parks or zoos and make your way to the beach.

En Route
Leaving Palm Springs you'll take Interstate 10 West to the 215 Freeway south, which eventually becomes the 15 Freeway. Off the 15 Freeway in Riverside County is **Temecula**, where a fledg-ling wine country is found as well as an historic old town with many shops and restaurants. Take the Rancho California Road exit toward Old Town Front Street. This will take you to Old Town Temecula.

As you continue south along the I-15, look for directional signs leading to San Diego. Highway 163 south will take you into downtown San Diego via 10th Avenue to Broadway.

In Town
The **Gaslamp Quarter** is a great place to begin your trip to San

Diego. While it's gotten a bit touristy in recent years, there is still a local vibe. The thrust of action is on 5th Street, but 4th and 6th Streets, which parallel 5th, are also packed with restaurants and clubs. Horton Plaza, a multi-level outdoor shopping esplanade, is also located in the Gaslamp Quarter near 4th and Broadway. To the east is **Petco Park**, home to the San Diego Padres, where you can take a tour of the stadium. You can continue south to the waterfront and head west towards Seaport Village for more shopping and street entertainment.

Take the ferry from downtown's **Broadway Pier** to Coronado Island, where you can disembark at **The Ferry Landing Market-place** and make your way to Orange Avenue, the island's main commercial district. Continue down Orange Avenue until you reach the **Hotel Del Coronado**, where you can wander the grounds or enjoy an afternoon drink at one of the waterfront lounges. If you don't want to take the ferry, you can also drive to Coronado Island via Interstate 5 south to the Coronado Bridge.

Explore some of the city's fun and funky little neighborhoods, such as **Little Italy, Hillcrest, Mission Beach** and **Pacific Beach.** These neighborhoods are where the locals live, work and play. If you're a history buff, then you'll want to visit **Old Town San Diego State Historical Park, Cabrillo National Park**, where the first European explorer landed in the 16th century, and the **USS Midway Aircraft Carrier Museum** – all detailed in the San Diego

chapter. **Balboa Park** is a great place to spend some time with its world-famous zoo, museums, and beautiful gardens.

You'll want to take advantage of the great outdoors and some of San Diego's seasonal events. If you're visit-ing between December and April, don't miss an opportunity to witness the migration of the California gray whales from the cold waters of Alaska to the warm waters of Baja, California, where they birth and rear their young. Many companies offer half-day excursions on the open seas to observe this fascinating phenomena where as many as 200 whales per day have been spotted off the San Diego coastline. San Diego Harbor Excursions is just one of many companies that offer seasonal **whale watching excursions**. *Info:* www.sdhe.com. Tel. 619/234-4111. Advanced reservations required.

You can also witness the migration from land at the **Cabrillo National Monument** situated on the picturesque Point Loma peninsula. The glass-enclosed observatory overlook allows you to scout for whales on solid ground. You can also explore whale exhibits and listen to a taped narration that describes these gigantic creatures characteristics. Afterwards, head to the park's tidepools. *Info:* www.nps.gov/cabr. Tel. 619/557-5450. Point Loma. 1800 Cabrillo Memorial Drive. Admission is $5.

From March to May is when the **Flower Fields of Carlsbad** display a full spectrum of vivid colors. This North County spectacle has taken place for more than 60 years transforming the rolling hills of Carlsbad into one of the most spectacular and color coordinated displays of natural beauty.  There are 50 acres of Giant Tecolote Ranunculus flowers in full bloom for only 6-8 weeks each year. *Info:* www.theflowerfields.com. Tel. 760/431-0352. Carlsbad. Open March-May daily from 9am-6pm. Admission is $9 adults, $5 children.

Another fun, seasonal event, from September through November, is the **Julian Apple Harvest**. Located in the eastern part of the county, Julian is a former mining town whose Main Street looks much the same as it did during the 19th century. During the apple harvest, you can enjoy the autumn foliage (Julian actually has four mild seasons), art shows, entertainment and seasonal foods, such as the apple pie and cider. *Info:* www.julianca.com. Tel. 760/765-1857.

Near Town
San Diego is often called the **Two Nation Vacation** because of its close proximity to Mexico. Downtown San Diego is only 17 miles from the border, so it makes for a perfect daytrip. The border city, Tijuana, is alive with activity both day and night, and you'll find duty-free shopping, dog racing, arts and culture, authentic Mexican food, and an energetic nightlife. **Avenida Revolucion** is the city's main thoroughfare, where the bulk of shops and restaurants are located. The easiest and most practical way to visit Tijuana is to take the San Diego Trolley to the border, which is about a 40-minute journey one way. *Info:* www.tijuanaonline.org.

ORANGE COUNTY
Three days in Orange County will give you time for the beach, a day at a theme park, and another day for shopping and sights.

En Route
The trip from San Diego to Orange County is a straight shot down Interstate 5 heading north. You can make a stop along the way to one of two historic missions, **Mission San Luis Rey** in Oceanside or the **Mission San Juan Capistrano** further up the freeway in San Juan Capistrano off the Ortega Highway exit.

If you're staying in **Dana Point** or **Laguna Beach**, exit Pacific Coast Highway from Interstate 5. If you're saying in **Newport Beach** or **Huntington Beach**, continue along the 5 Freeway to the 405 Freeway north and take the MacArthur or Jamboree exits for Newport Beach; and the Beach Boulevard exit further up for Huntington Beach. If your destination is Disneyland, continue on Interstate 5 to Anaheim.

Coastal Orange County

Any time spent along the Orange County coast is going to be relaxing and enjoyable. **Huntington Beach** is great if you like to surf, and there is always Main Street at the foot of the pier for shopping and dining. **Newport Beach** is also primed for surfing, but you can also get caught up in all the shopping venues, both in town and nearby, including **Fashion Island** and the village of Corona del Mar with **South Coast Plaza** just up the road.

Laguna Beach is an artists' colony with nearly a **hundred galleries**, an **art museum**, the annual **Pageant of the Masters** art event and the **Sawdust Festival,** where local artists display and sell their works, both events take place during the summer months. The beaches are great for surfing, as well as for exploring the tidepools. **Dana Point** is more of a sleepy town with great resorts and a full-service marina. Nearby is San Juan Capistrano and its magnificent mission.

Inland Orange County

Disneyland Resort is the main inland attraction and shouldn't be missed if you're traveling with children. There are now two parks, the original Disneyland and the neighboring California Adventure plus the free Downtown Disney shopping and entertainment district. If you have only one day, don't attempt both parks. Instead, enjoy the original theme park, which is ideal for first-time visitors, young children, and the young at heart.

A few other noteworthy attractions in these parts include the **Richard Nixon Library & Birthplace** in Yorba Linda; shopping and dining along the historic Orange Circle in **Old Town Orange**; and taking in a baseball game at **Angel Stadium** from April to October or catching a hockey game at the Honda Center where the **Anaheim Ducks** play – both are in Anaheim and the venues are separated only by the freeway. If you really like theme parks—or theme parks with thrilling rides—there is **Knott's Berry Farm** in Buena Park.

SANTA BARBARA

This should be the most relaxing part of your trip. You'll want to return home feeling rested rather than having to recuperate from a hectic, non-stop, must-see everything excursion. Take a day to wander through downtown and along the wharf, use another to visit the wineries and their tasting rooms, and be sure to visit a few of Santa Barbara's key attractions.

En Route

You'll travel from Orange County up the 405 Freeway North towards Los Angeles where you'll take the 101 Freeway towards Ventura.

If you are into politics, you may want to visit the **Ronald Reagan Presidential Library and Museum** in Simi Valley. From the 405 Freeway, you'll pass through LA's westside and continue to Highway 118 towards Simi Valley. Exit Madera Road South and turn right, then make another right on Madera Road to Presidential Drive. The library is at 40 Presidential Drive. This is the nation's largest and most elaborate presidential library with displays and exhibits that include a full-size replica of the Oval Office and a recreated White House State Dinner. You can also visit the President's memorial site where he was laid to rest on June 11, 2004. A recent addition to the library is **Air Force One**, sometimes referred to as the *Flying White House,* which served seven presidents, from President Kennedy to President George H.W. Bush, as well as countless national and foreign dignitaries. *Info:* www.reaganlibrary.net. Tel. 800/410-8354. Simi Valley. 40 Presidential Drive. Open daily 10am-5pm. Admission is $12 adults, $3 children.

Spend your first day in Santa Barbara along **State Street** and the waterfront. Visit the shops, boutiques and galleries as you make your way from Sola Street down to Stearns Wharf. If you feel like it, you'll have time to spend an hour or more at the **Santa Barbara**

Museum of Art or on a self-guided tour of the **Santa Barbara Courthouse**. Later in the day take a walk around the grounds of the **Mission Santa Barbara** and wander across the street to the Rose Garden. Be sure to return to your resort or inn in time for afternoon wine and cheese, an amenity offered complimentary at most hotels.

You'll want to take a day exploring **Santa Barbara's Wine Country**, about a 40 mile drive up Highway 154 or you can take the 101 Freeway north and exit Highway 246. You can spend the morning wandering through the shops of Solvang, a windmill-laden town settled by the Danish in the early 1900s, then set out for an afternoon along the wine trail. Either picnic at one of the vineyards, or enjoy lunch at the **Los Olivos Café** or the **Wine Cask,** both on Grand Avenue in Los Olivos.

If you have kids, make a point to visit the **Santa Barbara Zoo**. You'll also want to shop along Coast Village Road in Montecito, an exclusive Santa Barbara area. And, if you happen to be in town on a Saturday morning, wander around the **Farmers' Market**. Reserve Sunday morning for the **Arts & Crafts Fair** along the beach near Stearns Wharf.

9. BEST SLEEPS & EATS

Only the best options in each price category have made the cut. No need for you to waste your valuable time trying to decipher where to unpack your bags for a spell or what the best choices are for refueling. Keep in mind that Southern California has a high ratio of expensive hotels and the rule of thumb is this: You're likely to get a better nightly rate in urban areas (Los Angeles proper, Downtown San Diego) on weekends when business travelers have vacated the city. At the same time, if you book a stay at a hotel during the week (typically Sunday-Thursday) at some of the resort destinations, such as Santa Barbara, Coastal Orange County or Palm Springs, you may secure a lower rate than on the weekend. Summer rates are always higher than off-season rates as well, except in Palm Springs when it's considered low season due to triple-digit temperatures.

Expensive listings receive three dollar signs (rooms starting at $400 per night), **moderate** hotels get two (rates beginning at $175 nightly) and **budget** properties ($175 per night or less) earn just one.

LOS ANGELES

BEST SLEEPS
The Beverly Hills Hotel and Bungalows $$$

If one of the highlights of staying in Los Angeles is seeing a celebrity, then you've got to check into the historic Beverly Hills Hotel, also known as The Pink Palace. There are a number of secluded guest rooms, suites, and individual bungalows surrounded by 12 acres of lush gardens. The hotel's swimming pool is legendary with a row of neatly lined cabanas, while the Spa by La Prairie is the ultimate  in pampering. For dining there is The Polo Lounge (take your meal on the outdoor terrace) or The Fountain Coffee Shop, a spiffy soda fountain with just 20 pink bar stools. *Info:* www.thebeverlyhillshotel.com. Tel. 310/276-2251. Beverly Hills. 9641 Sunset Boulevard. 204 guest rooms and bungalows.

Is It Worth It?

Is a hotel really worth $400 or more a night? If you want to save money, call the hotel directly to secure the best possible rate, use online reservation systems, and check hotel websites for unadvertised specials. If you're planning on staying at a hotel for multiple days, ask for a discount. And don't forget about AAA discounts and rates for mature travelers.

Chateau Marmont $$$

Only a modest sign points towards the steep driveway to indicate that the Chateau Marmont exists. Its gothic castle-like façade, located off the Sunset Strip, is aptly shrouded. Built in 1929 as an upscale apartment complex, the building was quickly converted into a hotel after the stock market crashed a few months later. Steeped in Hollywood lore, Jean Harlow honeymooned here and John Belushi—who checked in, then checked out permanently

— overdosed on drugs behind the door of Bungalow #3. Accommodations include rooms and suites with balconies and kitchens, some even include fireplaces and grand pianos. Pets welcome, too. *Info:* www.chateaumarmont.com. Tel. 323/656-1010. West Hollywood. 8221 Sunset Boulevard. 54 rooms, suites and bungalows.

Loews Santa Monica Beach Hotel $$$
The soaring five-story glass atrium lobby belonging to this luxury hotel overlooks the sand and surf, making you want to just stay put there for hours. The guest rooms are located on the four floors above with each offering oversized bathrooms, contemporary furnishings and some rather spectacular views if you're on the ocean side – which is really the reason for staying here in the first place. There is a swimming pool on the lobby level, a pair of upscale restaurants, poolside dining and a relaxing spa. *Info:* www.santamonicaloewshotel.com Tel. 310/458-6700. Santa Monica. 1700 Ocean Avenue. 359 rooms and suites.

Shutters on the Beach $$$
Gracious coastal living best describes this resort, which, in my

humble opinion, is worth every cent so long as you have a room overlooking the beach. The shingled façade, whitewashed wooden balconies, vine-covered trellises, and striped awnings conceal fabulous guest rooms that are so inviting you simply won't want to leave. *Info:* www.shuttersonthebeach.com. Tel. 310/458-0030. Santa Monica. One Pico Boulevard. 198 rooms and suites.

Avalon Hotel $$
Is there anywhere in the LA vicinity that Marilyn Monroe did not live? The Avalon Hotel, a former apartment building that has been converted into a stylish retreat, is one of the blond bombshell's former cribs. The hotel is a cluster of three buildings with the best rooms overlooking the vintage hourglass-shaped pool. *Info:* www.avalonbeverlyhills.com. Tel. 310/277-5221. Beverly Hills. 9400 West Olympic Boulevard. 84 rooms and suites.

The Biltmore Hotel $$

The Biltmore Hotel, opened in 1923 at the corner of Fifth and Grand, is an L.A. landmark. It is the cornerstone of downtown LA's business, financial and cultural districts. The stunning Italian-Renaissance architecture offers ornate columns, gorgeous frescoes and grand European charm. Decades ago the Academy Awards were held in the hotel's Biltmore Bowl, and the hotel has served as a backdrop

for countless movies. Guest rooms are small, but elegant. Not to be missed is afternoon tea in the Rendevous Court. *Info:* www.millenniumhotels.com Tel. 213/624-1011. Downtown. 506 South Grand Avenue. 693 rooms and suites.

Chamberlain West Hollywood $$

The lobby of the Chamberlain, with its dim lighting and techno-style music, feels like a clubby lounge. The four-story structure is in an enviable location, cradled between the Sunset Strip and Santa Monica Boulevard. Each room features a fireplace and balcony, while select suites offer kitchenettes and separate sitting areas. It's LA, so you know there's going to be a rooftop pool complete with cabanas. *Info:* www.chamberlainwesthollywood.com. Tel. 310/657-7400. West Hollywood. 1000 Westmount Drive. 112 rooms and suites.

Fairmont Miramar Hotel $$

The century-old fig tree that fronts the entrance to the Fairmont Miramar casts an impressive shadow on the hotel's façade. The hotel, which opened in 1921, includes the Palisades Tower, built in 1924, and the more modern 10-story Ocean Tower. Nestled among tropical flowers, soaring palm trees and tranquil waterfalls are some of the original garden bungalows featuring French doors, private patios and fabulous views of the ocean. I like this hotel because of its convenient location — within walking distance to the ocean, pier, Third Street Promenade, and area attractions — as well as the Fairmont Hotel's trademark amenities and service. *Info:* www.fairmont.com/santamonica. Tel. 310/ 576-7777. Santa Monica. 101 Wilshire Boulevard. 302 rooms and suites.

Hilton Checkers Hotel $$

Just like its neighbor The Biltmore, the Hilton Checkers Hotel is also an historic 1920s property. Smaller in size with just 12 floors and 188 rooms, the Hilton Checkers is the only four-diamond boutique property in downtown. Rooms are very cozy with soothing color schemes and city views. The hotel features an award-winning restaurant, upscale bar, and an inviting patio area for dining. There is also a spa on the premises, and a breathtaking rooftop pool. *Info:* www.hiltoncheckers.com. Tel. 213/624-0000. Downtown. 535 South Grand Avenue. 188 rooms and suites.

Hollywood Roosevelt Hotel $$

A few years ago you could have stayed at this hotel for a song. While the asking price for an overnight stay has increased, so has the drama surrounding this Hollywood landmark. Fledgling and established stars arrive nightly to enjoy the velvet rope treatment courtesy of the Tropicana Poolside Bar. The rooms at this 1927 hotel, site of the very first Academy Awards, are now scene-stealers themselves having been completely revamped to offer A-listers and regular folk a luxurious setting. The Dakota *(see Best Eats Los Angeles)*, located on the premises, is an excellent place for dinner. The Roosevelt is across the street from Grauman's Chinese Theater, as well as the Hollywood and Highland shopping and entertainment center. *Info:* www.hollywoodroosevelt.com. Tel. 323/466-7000. Hollywood. 7000 Hollywood Boulevard. 302 rooms and suites.

Le Merigot $$

This JW Marriott Beach Hotel & Spa offers the perfect balance when it comes to luxury and budget. The hotel's understated elegance makes all guests feel comfortable, whether you're a soccer mom from Minnesota or a movie mogul from Malibu – even pets are made to feel at home. Some rooms have full ocean views and balconies, and others require a bit of a neck craning to see any water. There is a multi-level pool area and spa. The Santa Monica Pier and Third Street Promenade are also within walking distance. *Info:* www.lemerigothotel.com. Tel. 310/ 305-9700. Santa Monica. 1740 Ocean Avenue. 175 rooms and suites.

Luxe Hotel Sunset Boulevard $$

This luxury boutique hotel sits on seven secluded acres at the gateway to one of LA's most exclusive neighborhoods. Nearby is The Getty Center, which is easy to reach considering the hotel provides daily shuttle service to and from, as well as access to great shopping in both nearby Brentwood and Westwood, home to the UCLA campus. Split-level rooms, coated in a mix of crème, taupe and chocolate brown, are contemporary and streamlined and elegantly appointed with flat screen televisions, iPod stations positioned bedside, WiFi – you name it. There is a full-service spa on the premises, heated pool, tennis courts, a restaurant and lounge. *Info:* www.luxehotels.com. Tel. 310/476-6571. Bel Air. 11461 West Sunset Boulevard. 161 rooms and suites.

LA

Maison 140 $$

This 1930s hotel, located on a quiet street in Beverly Hills, was the former residence of silent screen star Lillian Gish. The outside looks a bit ordinary, but the inside pays homage to the classic Parisian pensiones of the last century with its French and Asian inspired décor. Guest rooms feature four-poster beds and enough amenities to warrant an extended stay. There's no swimming pool to speak of, but guests are granted permission to take a dip in the hour-glass swimming pool at the nearby Avalon (a sister property also listed as a Best Sleeps destination, above). Free breakfast and evening wine included. *Info:* www.maison140beverlyhills.com. Tel. 310/281-4000. Beverly Hills. 140 S. Lasky Drive. 45 rooms and suites.

Ritz-Carlton, Huntington Hotel & Spa $$

For many local residents, a stay at this hotel is a rite of passage. Steeped in history, the resort first opened in 1907. The residential location, in an established "old" money part of Pasadena, is about a 20 minute drive from downtown Los Angeles. Rooms are housed in the original main building, and there are a handful of freestanding bungalows. There is a pair of restaurants, a lounge, afternoon tea, a swimming pool, and luxurious spa. *Info:* www.ritzcarlton.com/hotels/huntington. Tel. 626/585-6434.

Pasadena. 1401 South Oak Knoll Avenue. 392 guest rooms and suites.

Best Western Sunset Plaza $

If you want to stay near the trendy hot spots of Hollywood without blowing your entire vacation budget, then the Best Western Sunset Plaza should be on your short list. You're right on the Sunset Strip — amid the glitz and glamour — next door to the very expensive Argyle Hotel. The guest rooms wraparound a courtyard, and there is a swimming pool offering million-dollar views. A recent renovation yields some rather nicely appointed accommodations, and suite accommodations include balconies, additional bedrooms and kitchenettes. A complimentary continental breakfast is included in the rate. *Info:* www.bestwestern.com Tel. 323/654-0750. Hollywood. 8400 Sunset Boulevard. 100 rooms and suites.

Casa Malibu Inn $

The Casa Malibu Inn doesn't try to keep up with the Joneses nor does it put on any airs, it has stayed true to its 1920s roots as an intimate hideaway and that's what makes it special. There's no pool, but it's the only hotel in Malibu with its own private beach. The Catalina Suite is the former digs of actress Lana Turner. This is a real affordable find and would make a great escape for a romantic getaway. *Info:* no website. Tel. 310/456-2219. Malibu. 22752 Pacific Coast Highway. 21 rooms and suites.

Farmer's Daughter $

Not all facelifts bode well in La La Land. Just look at a few aging celebrities who have braved the knife. The Farmer's Daughter,

 named for its close proximity to the famed Farmers Market, has never looked better. The once rundown motel has gone from drab to fab. You'll find a pool, cabanas, and restaurant on the premises aptly named TART (could this be an ode to the farmer's daughter?) What makes this hotel "best worthy" is its location and price – both are

unbeatable. *Info:* www.farmersdaughterhotel.com. Tel. 323/937-3930. Fairfax District. 115 South Fairfax. 66 rooms.

Hotel Angeleno $
Located at the crossroads of the moneyed Brentwood (OJ Simpson's former neighborhood) and the exclusive area of Bel Air, Hotel Angeleno is the closest hotel to The Getty Center. There are 16 floors containing spacious and modernly appointed guest rooms, each with its own private balcony – request a room that doesn't face the freeway. There is a spectacular penthouse-level restaurant and lounge boasting stunning views. You could easily use the hotel as a home base to explore the rest of Southern California. *Info:* www.jdvhospitality.com. Tel. 310/476-6411. Brentwood. 170 North Church Lane. 209 rooms and suites.

Ramada Plaza Hotel West Hollywood $
I am quick to recommend this hotel to those on a budget. The location is great, rooms are well appointed, and the price is right considering you're staying in the heart of West Hollywood. The area also caters to a large gay population, hence the nickname Boys Town. In addition to its bulk of standard Art Deco inspired rooms, the Ramada Plaza features many deluxe suites and lofts that offer ample space. The hotel's pool is laptop friendly with free wireless Internet access, and pets are also welcomed guests. Step outside the hotel door onto Santa Monica Boulevard (part of Route 66), and you're within walking distance to some great shops and restaurants. *Info:* www.ramada-wh.com. Tel. 310/652-6400. West Hollywood. 8585 Santa Monica Boulevard. 221 rooms and suites.

The Standard Downtown $
File this one under hip hotels. The Standard Downtown is über cool, from its minimalist décor to its vibrant use of color. The clientele is a mix of models, actors and wannabes. Rooms convey a mid-century chic with platform beds and a few oddities, such as a giant rubber foot in the bathrooms of certain abodes. The rooftop bar and pool is one of the most desirable locations to see and be seen – the party begins as soon as the sun goes down. *Info:* www.standardhotel.com. Tel. 213/892-8080. 550 South Flower Street. Downtown. 205 rooms and suites.

LA

BEST EATS

Café La Boheme $$$

Named for the Puccuni opera, the setting at Café La Boheme is

 equal parts gothic and theatric though a recent revamp has somewhat sedated the original Transylvania decor. The service is stellar and the food is excellent with an emphasis on fresh fish, pasta, risotto and aged steak. The restaurant's lounge, Bar Tosca, offers a limited and more casual menu. *Info:* www.café-laboheme.com. Tel. 323/848-2360. West Hollywood. 8400 Santa Monica Boulevard.

Dakota $$$

This swank and very modern steakhouse is located inside the historic Hollywood Roosevelt Hotel. Guests enter from either the grand staircase or hotel lobby before being met by a sophisticated mix of chocolate browns, ambient lighting, and a fleet of suede and leather banquettes. The bar, located inside the main dining room, is extremely sexy with a clientele to match. The restaurant serves breakfast, lunch and dinner, but it's the dinner setting that really dazzles the senses. *Info:* www.dakota-restaurant.com. Tel. 323/ 769-8888. Hollywood. 7000 Hollywood Boulevard.

The Ivy $$$

Today's hostess is tomorrow's star, just ask Ashley Judd who used to do the seating honors at this venerable LA eatery. The bungalow setting and white picket fence, surrounded by more contemporary buildings, looks almost like a movie set and there are enough celebrities dining here to fill the pages of *People* magazine. The food is generously portioned and, dare we say, pricey? Still, the classic chopped salad, plump crab cakes and other assortment of comfort foods, coupled with the star power that be, make The Ivy the quintessential LA dining experience. *Info:* Tel. 310/274-8303. West Los Angeles. 113 Roberston Boulevard.

The Lobster $$$
The original Lobster first crawled on the scene in 1923 before
closing its doors in 1984. But everyone loves a comeback, so The
Lobster returned bigger and better in the late 1990s. Located at the
entrance to the Santa Monica Pier, the space is a modern marvel of
glass, steel and wood with spectacular views from most tables –
especially those on the terrace overlooking the ocean and pier. The
lunch and dinner menus change daily because the restaurant
specializes in fresh fish. Both the food and service are enjoyable, as
are those million-dollar vistas. *Info:* www.thelobster.com. Tel.
310/ 458-9294. Santa Monica. 1602 Ocean Avenue.

Musso & Frank's $$$
No trip to Hollywood would be complete without stopping in for
at least a drink to Musso & Frank's. Many famous dining haunts
from Hollywood's Golden Age, like the Brown Derby and
Chasen's, are just distant memories. Somehow Musso & Frank's,
the oldest restaurant in Tinseltown having been established in
1919, has withstood the test of time and fickle tastes. It's packed
with sentimental value and a menu of Continental standards
delivered by career waiters to big leather banquettes. The
restaurant is still frequented by celebrities and, rumor has it, that
Al Pacino likes to dine at table 28. *Info:* Tel. 323/467-7788.
Hollywood. 6667 Hollywood Boulevard.

The Polo Lounge $$$
For the longest time I was intimidated to dine at The Polo Lounge
inside the Beverly Hills Hotel. It had a reputation as an industry-
only hangout where actors and agents were doted on by the wait
staff, and the unrecognizable were relegated to tables by the
kitchen door. Not true. The restaurant, especially the bougainvillea-
draped verandah, offers one of the
nicest settings in Los Angeles and
the staff is very accommodating to
everyone. The restaurant is open for
breakfast, lunch and dinner. The
menu features everything from
sandwiches and Kobe-style burgers
for lunch, to rack of lamb and New

LA

York steak for dinner. A star sighting is almost guaranteed. *Info:* www.thebeverlyhillshotel.com. Tel. 310/ 276-2251. Beverly Hills. 9641 Sunset Boulevard.

The Restaurant at Hotel Bel-Air $$$

This is one of the city's most romantic settings, and the menu is

a blend of haute French and California cuisine. Open for breakfast, lunch and dinner, the seasonal menu never disappoints. There are two dining areas: The formal dining room located inside, or the al fresco terrace draped in colorful bougainvillea. One option that allows you to enjoy the setting without spending a lot of money is the daily afternoon tea, which takes place Monday-Saturday. Reservations are a must. *Info:* www.hotelbelair.com. Tel. 310/ 472-1211. Bel Air. 701 Stone Canyon Road.

ABC Seafood $$

Dim Sum, which means *delights of the heart*, has always been a popular treat in Los Angeles' Chinese neighborhood. ABC Seafood serves dim sum the traditional way with Chinese women maneuvering carts, which display an array of meat dumplings and other little bites, about the room. Fish dishes are first shown to you live, then brought back to you on a plate once the kitchen staff has transformed them into menu items. The staff here is very skilled and will anticipate your every need. *Info:* Tel. 213/680-2887. Downtown/Chinatown. 205 Ord Street.

Bin 8945 $$

It seems like wine bars are popping up faster than Starbucks these days, especially in Los Angeles. These new dining destinations, such as Bin 8945, offer small plates, flights of wine, and stylish settings. There are nearly 60 wines offered by the glass all selected to complement the menu of oysters, empanadas, fresh fish and market dishes. *Info:* bin8945.com. Tel. 310/550-8945. West Hollywood. 8945 Santa Monica Boulevard.

Border Grill $$

Celebrity chefs Susan Feniger and Mary Sue Milliken, better known as the *Too Hot Tamales*, are the creators of this boisterous, piñata-colored Mexican restaurant. The restaurant features a menu of creative Mexican fare, such as roasted lamb tacos or the gaucho steak with caramelized onions. The tortilla soup is excellent, and the guacamole is great with chips or as an enhancement to many of the dishes. Shaken margaritas are a specialty. Brunch served weekends. *Info:* www.bordergrill.com. Tel. 310/451-1655. Santa Monica. 1445 Fourth Street.

LA

Campanile $$

This gourmet restaurant is packed during its weekly Thursday Grilled Cheese Night, which features a dozen variations of the childhood classic. Housed in what were to be Charlie Chaplin's offices (he lost the building in his divorce settlement to first wife Lita Grey), Campanile packs a rather hip crowd inside its inviting—but noisy—dining room. Owner and Chef Mark Peel prepares an eclectic menu of perfectly seasoned pasta, rabbit and seafood. Breads are delivered fresh from La Brea Bakery next door. *Info:* www.campanilerestaurant.com. Tel. 323/938-1447. 624 South La Brea Avenue. West Los Angeles.

Dan Tana's $$

Behind the doors of this yellow bungalow is where agents, actors, and producers are brokering deals for the next big blockbuster movie. The big red, leatherette booths and dangling Chianti bottles help to create an unpretentious mood despite the power clientele. The menu is strictly old-school Italian: spaghetti and meatballs, manicotti and some serious ravioli. The drinks (highballs, anyone?) are ample sized. *Info:* www.dantanasrestaurant.com. Tel. 310/275-9444. West Hollywood. 9071 Santa Monica Boulevard.

Engine Co. No. 28 $$

Housed in an actual 1912 firehouse, Engine Co. No. 28 is reminiscent of the classic grills you're likely to find in San Francisco or New York. The interiors feature large mahogany booths, a granite bar, original press tin ceilings and brick flooring. The sounds of Ella Fitzgerald, Frank Sinatra or Dean Martin are typical. The menu, inspired by firehouses around the country, is

LA

American comfort food: burgers, meatloaf, salads, club sandwiches, fresh fish and really decadent desserts. Reservations recommended. *Info:* www.engineco.com. Tel. 213/624-6996. Downtown. 644 South Figueroa Street.

Off Vine $$

The bungalow setting, Adirondack chairs and milky white walls set the mood at this quiet Hollywood retreat on Leland Way just off Vine, hence the name. Dining takes place inside the cottage, on the front porch or patio. Open daily for lunch and dinner, as well as on weekends for brunch, the eclectic menu ranges from sandwiches and salads to shrimp and steak. *Info:* www.offvine.com. Tel. 323/962-1900. Hollywood. 6263 Leland Way.

Formosa Café $

The crimson colored building and Confucius-style letter that spells out the café's name have been turning heads since 1934. The Cantonese-style menu has some new twists with items like the sesame and wasabi fries, and Asian paella. *Info:* www.formosacafe.com. Tel. 323/850-9050. West Los Angeles. 7156 Santa Monica Boulevard.

Miceli's $

While many time-honored establishments have closed, the 60-year-old Miceli's has managed to survive. Using family recipes smuggled from Sicily by way of Chicago, this family-owned restaurant just off Hollywood Boulevard offers delicious Italian cooking at very reasonable prices. In addition to wine and beer, the restaurant also offers a full bar and nightly entertainment. *Info:* www.micelisrestaurant.com. Tel. 323/466-3438. Hollywood. 1646 N. Las Palmas.

The Original Pantry Café $

If you want to make your first meal of the day a memorable one, stop by The Pantry. Opened in 1924, the restaurant, owned by former LA mayor Richard Riordan, is now housed in two buildings and diners are seated on a first come, first-served basis. The menu board lists the basics: eggs, potatoes, pork chops, steak, bacon or sausage. Bring cash; as credit cards are not accepted. *Info:*

www.pantrycafe.com. Tel. 213/972-9279. Downtown. 877 South Figueroa Street.

Philippe's, The Original $

Opened in 1908 (the original location was a few blocks away and demolished in the 1950s to make room for the Freeway), this is where the French dip sandwich was invented. Ordering takes place at a long counter where the lines are usually several people deep. The sandwiches are made to order (ask for yours to be double dipped in the au jus, a request not found on the menu board), and there is a display of salads, pickled eggs, pigs' feet and desserts. A cup of coffee will run you a dime. Cash only, and it's customary to leave a 10% tip for the sandwich maker. *Info:* www.philippes.com. Tel. 213/628-3781. Downtown. 1001 N. Alameda Street.

Pink's Hot Dogs $

Another Los Angeles culinary landmark, this hot dog stand has stood near the corner of La Brea and Melrose since 1939. The cramped white and red stucco building draws long lines along the boulevard and for good reason: the dogs are to die for. Pink's is famous for its chilidogs, but you can top your dog countless ways. The cramped dining room is covered with photos of celebrities also addicted to Pink's. This is a favorite haunt of Roseanne Barr, and  legend has it that Sean Penn proposed to Madonna at Pink's. Cash only. *Info:* www.pinkshollywood.com. Tel. 323/931-4223. Hollywood. 709 North La Brea Avenue.

Toast $

This hip little eatery on the Westside of town is exceptionally good. Dogs dine alongside their owners beneath a fleet of umbrella-shaded tables. This casual restaurant is open for breakfast, but it's their lunch offerings that are the most creative. The menu features various soups, chopped salads, quiche, baguette sandwiches and wraps. *Info:* www.toastbakerycafe.com. West Los Angeles. Tel. 323/655-5018. 8221 West 3rd Street. West Los Angeles.

SAN DIEGO

BEST SLEEPS
Rancho Valencia Resort $$$

This Mission-style resort, draped in fragrant blossoms and  cascading bougainvillea, features ample-sized cottages with private entrances and their own secluded patios, outdoor whirlpools, fireplaces, and bathrooms that might be mistaken for separate living quarters – they're huge. The new Grove Suites are a complement to the resort's original design and are equally luxurious. Amenities include an outdoor swimming pool, spa services, and tennis. *Info:* www.ranchovalencia.com. Tel. 858/756-1123. Rancho Santa Fe. 5921 Valencia Circle. 49 rooms and suites.

Crystal Pier Hotel and Cottages $$

This hotel has no restaurant, no spa, and no concierge. What it does have is a swimming pool as big as an ocean. That's because the swimming pool *is* the ocean as the Crystal Pier Hotel and Cottages does an amazing balancing act above the blue Pacific. It's not really a hotel at all, but a collection of vintage blue and white clapboard cottages that line the pier. Each cottage comes equipped with a kitchen and patio complete with ocean sprays and a single parking spot on the pier. Unless you're sleeping on a boat or floating on a raft, you can't get more "waterfront" than this. *Info:* www.crystalpier.com. Tel. 800/748-5894. Pacific Beach. 4500 Ocean Boulevard. 29 individual cottages.

Estancia La Jolla Hotel & Spa $$

Located across from the UC San Diego campus, this former

equestrian estate features low-rise buildings, Spanish architecture and breathtaking gardens. The collection of rooms, scattered among three stories and built around a pair of courtyards, offers a welcoming escape. There is a pool, spa, and three restaurants including the pub-like Mustang & Burros, a rustic setting with indoor and outdoor fireplaces. *Info:* www.estancialajolla.com. Tel. 858/550-5000. La Jolla. 9700 N. Torrey Pines Road. 210 rooms and suites.

Hotel Del Coronado $$

It's been said that former Coronado Island resident and acclaimed writer L. Frank Baum used The Del, with its white gingerbread

façade and crimson turrets, as the inspiration for the Emerald City in his *Wizard of Oz* series. The Del is a classic and timeless treasure that must be experienced at least once in a lifetime. Guest rooms are housed in either the original hotel or the newer, more contemporary buildings. Rooms range in size from small to spacious with an equal range of views — or no views — to match. The first phase of a 15-year master plan has just been completed. It includes the addition of The Spa at the Del, a 20,000 square-foot luxury spa; the Beach Village, featuring 78 exclusive ocean view guest rooms and suites literally encapsulated in their own village; and a new fitness center. *Info:* www.hoteldel.com. Tel. 619/435-6611. Coronado Island. 1500 Orange Avenue.

Hotel Parisi $$

Located on a prominent corner in the heart of La Jolla's seaside village, the Zen-like Hotel Parisi is an all-suite hotel occupying the entire second floor of a two-story retail building. Located on a main street across from the beach, Hotel Parisi embraces the Chinese art of feng shui with guest rooms thoughtfully designed to create balance and harmony. Hues of ebony and crisp white are infused with splashes of red. Rooms feature walkout balconies, and the popular in-room spa treatments are booked well in advance. *Info:* www.hotelparisi.com. Tel. 858/454-1511. La Jolla. 1111 Prospect. 28 rooms and suites.

Hotel Solamar $$

With the addition of Petco Park, home of the San Diego Padres, downtown San Diego has suddenly taken a turn for the trendy. Swank hotels and hip little eateries are more abundant than ever before. One of the newer additions to the cityscape is Hotel Solamar, a Kimpton property located in the heart of the Gaslamp Quarter near the ballpark. Rooms are sophisticated, yet playful, with beds cloaked in duvets covered in giant chocolate brown and aqua polka dots. The fourth floor is like a playground for adults. The outdoor setting features a pool, cabanas, fire pits and the J6Bar. Free morning coffee and evening wine included. The hotel is pet friendly, too. *Info:* www.hotelsolamar.com. Tel. 619/531-8740. Gaslamp District. 435 Sixth Avenue. 235 rooms and suites.

La Costa Resort and Spa $$

Located in the coastal foothills of Carlsbad on a 400-acre sprawl, La Costa has kept its hold as one of the most celebrated resorts and spas in the world. The resort recently completed a top-to-bottom, multi-million-dollar redevelopment that has resulted in a new spa, completely remodeled guest rooms, a new clubhouse and fitness center, and a pair of new restaurants. No dollar was spared as both of La Costa's two championship golf courses also received major facelifts. The resort also rolls out the red carpet for families by offering a new kids club program and facility, as well as a room just for teens with an X-Box gaming lounge, pool tables and air hockey. LegoLand is just minutes away. *Info:* www.lacosta.com. Tel. 760/438-9111. Carlsbad. 2100 Costa Del Mar Road. 511 rooms and suites.

The Lodge at Torrey Pines $$

The architects and designers did a superb job of creating an Arts and Crafts-style resort for the 21st century. The Lodge at Torrey Pines looks as if it were plucked from the past, except with all the modern amenities you want and expect. The lobby is warm and inviting with great views of the pool and cabanas in the foreground and the lush fairways in the distance. The rooms have a warm, cozy feel and are dressed in earthy tones, while the entire lodge (rooms, hallways, lobby, etc.) is infused with the faint scent of pine. There is a lovely restaurant on the premises where jackets are required in the evening, and a more casual lounge for cocktails. The resort, near the campus of UC San Diego, overlooks the heralded Torrey Pines Public Golf Course, a stop on the PGA Golf Tour. *Info:* www.lodgeattorreypines.com. Tel. 858/ 453-4420. 11480 North Torrey Pines Road. La Jolla. 171 rooms and suites.

San Diego

Paradise Point $$

Overlooking Mission Bay near SeaWorld, Paradise Point has an isolated feel as it sits on a private 44-acre island. Lush tropical landscaping, a platinum stretch of beach, and serene water features surrounds the fleet of low-slung bungalows. Each single-level abode boasts a lanai and relaxing views. The resort also features a bay front restaurant that serves fresh seafood, and a bar and grill known for its live music and patio dancing. There is also a spa on the premises. The location is certainly geared towards families with Belmont Park, SeaWorld and Mission Beach all nearby. *Info:* www.paradisepoint.com. Tel. 858/ 274-4630. Mission Bay. 1404 Vacation Road.

Tower 23 Hotel $$

By all accounts, Pacific Beach is the quintessential surf ghetto. When Tower 23 Hotel, named for the neighboring lifeguard beacon, opened its doors a couple of years ago, suddenly PB (as it's known to locals) got a shot of sophistication. It's the only luxury, lifestyle hotel located on the beach. Its boxy, transparent design and minimalist approach is a departure from the typical beach resorts found in Southern California. The rooms and suites use hues and elements that reflect the beachfront setting. If you want to combine sightseeing with some serious downtime, this hotel is ideal because of its beachfront location. *Info:* tower23hotel.com. Tel. 858/270-2323. Pacific Beach. 723 Felspar Street. 44 rooms and suites.

U.S. Grant Hotel $$

After its recent acquisition by a Native American tribe, this early 20th-century hotel, managed by Starwood Hotel and Resorts, underwent a much-needed renovation that resulted in a two-year closure. What was unveiled was an extremely upscale look that had been previously absent. The lobby, where afternoon tea has been a century-old tradition, is elegantly appointed. The tranquil rooms are plush and inviting with clean lines and stylish furnishings. An emphasis on service is also in place, and in-room spa treatments are available for the first time in the hotel's history. *Info:* www.usgrant.net. 619/232-3121. Downtown. 326 Broadway. 270 rooms and suites.

W San Diego $$

The W Hotel brand tends to be very grown up, yet playful at the same time. The W San Diego, located in a transitional neighborhood not far from the Gaslamp Quarter. The lobby doubles as a living room with seating arrangements designed to promote conversation. The rooms above are small and trendy with plenty of hi-tech gadgets and Bliss body products. The rooftop beach bar, with its heated sandy floor, is home to private cabanas and an outdoor fireplace. *Info:* www.starwoodhotels.com. Tel. 619/398-3100. Downtown. 421 West B Street. 261 rooms and suites.

El Cordova Hotel $

Everyone wants to stay at the Hotel del Coronado, but not everyone has the budget. For those who want to stay on Coronado, I suggest you have a nightcap at The Del and stay at El Cordova Hotel. Located down the street from The Del amid the island's shopping district, this best-kept secret is both charming and affordable. It was originally built in 1902 as a country mansion and was eventually transformed into a Spanish village. Rooms vary with appointments, from hardwood floors and sitting areas to full-size kitchens. *Info:* www.elcordovahotel.com. Tel. 619/ 432-4131. Coronado Island. 1351 Orange Avenue. 40 rooms and suites.

La Pensione Hotel $

This simple, European-style hotel located in the heart of San Diego's Little Italy, just blocks from the Gaslamp Quarter and waterfront, is a real bargain. A room for two on the weekend is less than $100 per night. Established in 1991 and renovated in 2003, the hotel features small, but nice rooms with the quietest of the lot overlooking the hotel courtyard. All rooms can only accommodate two guests, so families should look elsewhere. The hotel has two restaurants and there are great culinary destinations all over Little Italy. For the price and location, this inn is unbeatable. *Info:* lapensionehotel.com. Tel. 619/236-8000. Little Italy. 606 West Date Street. 79 rooms.

Les Artistes Inn $

This funky and unconventional inn is located in the village of Del Mar, just north of La Jolla. This once shabby 1930s motel is now an artistic retreat. Spanish in style, the two-story structure sits at the bottom of a slope on the south side of the street. There are no views to really speak of, but you don't really notice because creativity abounds. The theme rooms are named for artists, from Diego Rivera to Georgia O'Keefe. The beach is within walking distance, as well as shops and restaurants. The Del Mar Racetrack, which is open during the late summer, is a few minutes away by car. *Info:* www.lesartistesinn.com. Tel. 858/755-4646. Del Mar. 944 Camino Del Mar. 10 rooms.

Manchester Grand Hyatt San Diego $

This is Southern California's largest and tallest hotel offering endless conveniences. For starters, there are four restaurants, a spa, tennis courts and an outdoor swimming pool. Add to the mix its location, which is within walking distance to the Gaslamp Quarter and Seaport Village. The rooms are also very nicely appointed with panoramic views

San
Diego

of the city or harbor, marble baths, luxurious bedding, stereos with iPod docking capabilities, and work stations. *Info:* manchestergrand.hyatt.com. Tel. 619/232-1234. 1 Market Place. Downtown Waterfront. 1625 rooms and suites.

BEST EATS
Chez Loma $$$

Intimate dining is found in this 1889 Victorian home now belonging to Chez Loma. Located down the road from the Hotel del Coronado in the heart of the island's village, Chez Loma features a seasonal French menu of seafood, duck, lamb, foie gras, and pate. The wine list is extensive, and the restaurant also has an impressive martini menu and full bar. *Info:* www.chezloma.com. Tel. 619/435-0661. Coronado Island. 1132 Loma Avenue

Jake's Del Mar $$$

This beachfront restaurant is a favorite among locals for both its setting and cuisine. Floor-to-ceiling windows provide a panorama of the Pacific Ocean. The menu is a display of California coastal cuisine featuring fresh fish and shellfish with steak and chop options for landlubbers. Jake's is pricey, so if you want to enjoy the views but not an expensive meal, opt for a drink in the lively bar at sunset and order from the lounge menu. *Info:* www.jakesdelmar.com. Tel. 858/755-2002. Del Mar. 1660 Coast Boulevard.

Mille Fleurs $$$

Located in the heart of the quaint village of Rancho Santa Fe, this cozy restaurant is consistently named one of the top restaurants in the nation for both its food and ambiance. The menu, which changes daily, is a mélange of salads, pork, quail, seafood and pasta. The ambiance is a collection of intimate niches where the warmth of the fireplace creates a romantic setting. *Info:* www.millefleurs.com. Tel. 858/756-3085. North County – Rancho Santa Fe. 6009 Paseo Delicias.

Bella Luna $$

Tucked among the Gaslamp Quarter's fleet of restaurants is this delicious Italian bistro. This family-owned trattoria is intimate

with just a handful of tables both inside and along the sidewalk patio plus a few seats at the cozy bar. The menu, mostly regional
dishes from the island of Capri, is a mix of antipasti, pasta, fish and fabulous risotto dishes. The wine list features vintages from France, Italy and the Napa Valley region with more than two-dozen offered by the glass. *Info:* www.sandiegorestaurants.com/ bellaluna. Tel. 619/232-8844. Gaslamp Quarter. 728 Fifth Avenue.

Café Sevilla $$

This lively Spanish eatery is a spicy little number located in the Gaslamp Quarter where 40 varieties of traditional Spanish tapas and an array of paella dishes dominate the menu. You'll also find a cheese course, olive plates, bocadillos (Spanish sandwiches) and fruity pitchers of sangria. Things heat up on weekend nights when flamenco dancers take to the stage and the dinner show gets underway. *Info:* www.cafesevilla.com. Tel. 619/233-5979. Gaslamp Quarter. 555 Fourth Street.

Dakota Grill & Spirits $$

This casual and upscale restaurant is always packed to capacity. There are two floors for dining, as well as an upstairs bar with live piano music on weekends. Specialties of the house are mesquite grilled steaks and an assortment of fresh seafood. If you're considering dining in the Gaslamp Quarter, Dakota Grill should definitely be at the top of your list. *Info:* www.cohenrestaurants.com. Tel. 619/234-5554. Gaslamp Quarter. 901 Fifth Avenue.

Fresco Trattoria $$

Located in the village of Carlsbad is this charming and romantic family-owned restaurant. A scattering of tables, a roaring fireplace and a menu of Italian specialties makes for an enjoyable lunch or dinner. Some signature dishes include the shrimp bisque soup and gnocchi topped with creamy pesto sauce. The menu and wine list are extensive, and there is a children's menu as well. *Info:* www.fresco-trattoria.com. Tel. 760/720-3737. Carlsbad. 264 Carlsbad Village Dr.

San Diego

Indigo Grill $$
One of the most creative restaurants in San Diego, Indigo Grill is bold and daring. Noted for its intense flavors and dramatic décor, the menu takes you from the arctic region to the south of Mexico. Entrees run the gamut from blueberry-lacquered rack of lamb to apple-smoked pork ribs and wild mushroom ravioli. Indigo Grill is a definite standout in Little Italy. *Info:* www.cohnrestaurants.com. Tel. 619/234-6802. Little Italy. 1536 India Street.

Kemo Sabe $$
The dramatic décor, Pacific Rim menu and selection of local microbrews is enough reason to book a reservation at this fun and sometimes funky Hillcrest outpost. As the menu states, there is "dim sum and then sum" with a variety of fabulous appetizers. Great food and ambiance, plus more than 50 varieties of wine. *Info:* www.cohnrestaurants.com. Tel. 619/220-6802. Hillcrest. 3958 Fifth Avenue.

La Vache $$
With a nod to the old country, this French restaurant in San Diego's hip Hillcrest neighborhood offers a casual dining experience. The regional menu, served for lunch, dinner and weekend breakfasts, features simple ingredients and presentation. There is a long list of appetizers, French pizzas, salads, pasta and seafood dishes plus a signature onion soup that's excellent. For breakfast, there are omelets and crepes, plus café au lait served traditional style in a bowl. *Info:* www.lavacheandco.com. Tel. 619/295-0217. Hillcrest. 420 Robinson Ave.

Yard House $$
Known for its American fusion fare, classic rock music, and 130 taps of draft beer, Yard House features more than 100 menu items, including appetizers, salads, sandwiches, steaks, chops, pasta and seafood with an emphasis on presentation and generous portions. Downstairs is a living room-style lounge that caters to a young and hip crowd on weekends. *Info:* www.yardhouse.com. Tel. 619/233-YARD. Gaslamp Quarter. 1023 Fourth Avenue.

Café Pasta Pronto $
Located behind a McDonald's in a strip mall of all places is this

gem of a restaurant. Up front is the bakery case and a little narrow
passage way that leads to a few tables in the rear of the restaurant.
The menu features a large assortment of salads, quiche, sandwiches, pasta and desserts. Eat on the premises or take it to go to
enjoy either in your hotel room (ideal if you're staying in Del Mar
or Rancho Santa Fe) or for a picnic on the beach. *Info:* Tel. 858/481-
6017. Del Mar. 2673 Via De La Valle.

The Cottage $

Housed in one of La Jolla's original turn-of-the-century cottages,
this popular bistro features some serious comfort foods for
breakfast and lunch. The best seats are those under the umbrella-
shaded tables on the restaurant's front porch. Breakfast has all
the usual trappings — eggs, omelets and griddle dishes — with
some unusual twists. There are also some grab and go items, such
as muffins and cinnamon rolls. For lunch it's a mix of soup, salad,
and sandwiches plus fish tacos, pot pies and some other filling
dishes. *Info:* www.cottagelajolla.com. Tel. 858/454-8409. La Jolla.
7702 Fay Avenue.

Kansas City BBQ $

Consistently voted the best barbecue in San Diego, Kansas City
BBQ is also famous for having been one of the locations sites for
the 1986 Tom Cruise film *Top Gun*. The little white shack, with its
red awnings and blue umbrella-covered tables, offers a meaty
menu of ribs, chicken and steak coupled with some excellent
sauces. Best of all, when many of the area's restaurants are closed,
Kansas City BBQ stays open until 1am. *Info:* www.kcbbq.net. Tel.
619/231-9680. Downtown. 610 West Market Street.

Point Loma Seafoods $

This fish market, located right on the water, is also a casual
restaurant. The fish is as fresh as
you'll find because the owners
bring it in daily. On the menu is
fish, fish and more fish. Crab
cakes, shrimp salad, scallop
dishes, chowder bowls, and so
on. restaurant closes at 6:30pm,
so this is a better choice for a late

lunch. *Info:* www.pointlomaseafoods.com. Tel. 619/223-1109. Point Loma. 2805 Emerson Street.

Rubio's Fish Tacos!

Although they originated in San Felipe, Mexico, **fish tacos** are considered a San Diego specialty. Ralph Rubio brought his fish taco recipe back with him after a trip to the Baja Peninsula, and opened his very first fish taco stand in Mission Bay in the early 1980s. Today **Rubio's** has 150 locations in five states, but nothing is quite as good as the original location, which is still open at 4504 E. Mission Bay Drive.

The Turquoise Café Bar Europa $

You must be 21 and over to enjoy this stylish European café, which recreates the feeling of a small, local bar typical of southern Europe. You're welcome to order just coffee and a pastry or a complete meal and glass of wine. The menu is long, but simple with items such as marinated olives, prosciutto and melon, and a classic meat and cheese course. There are also panini sandwiches and more substantial meals, such as pasta and top sirloin. *Info:* www.cafeturquoise.com. Tel. 858/488-4200. Pacific Beach. 873 Turquoise Street.

JULIAN / ANZA-BORREGO

Julian Gold Rush Hotel $
A Victorian-era inn containing 15 rooms and cottages, this is the oldest continuously operating hotel in all of Southern California. Nightly rates include a full breakfast and afternoon tea. *Info:* www.julianhotel.com. Tel. 760/765-0201.

Borrego Valley Inn $
Located within Anza-Borrego Desert State Park, Borrego Valley Inn is an intimate adobe-style retreat. *Info:*www.borregovalleyinn.com. Tel. 760/767-0311. Another choice in the park is **La Casa Del Zorro**, the area's only full-service resort (www.lacasadelzorro.com, Tel. 760/767-5323).

ORANGE COUNTY

BEST SLEEPS

Balboa Bay Club & Resort $$$

With a 15-acre spread overlooking Newport Bay, The Balboa Bay Club & Resort is Newport Beach's only full-service waterfront resort. The resort resembles an Italian villa and is built on a trio of levels sharing the same bay front address as the 57-year-old Balboa Bay Club, whose guests and members once included John Wayne, Ronald and Nancy Reagan, Humphrey Bogart and Natalie Wood. Accommodations are roomy and offer patios with chaise lounges, sunken bathtubs, and added touches, such as refrigerators stocked with your choice of refreshments and snacks. Other perks include the use of the private beach, two swimming pools, a spa and plenty of sporty activities. *Info:* www.balboabayclub.com. Tel. 949/645-5000. Newport Beach. 1221 West Coast Highway. 160 guest rooms and suites.

Montage Resort & Spa $$$

The Montage is nothing short of spectacular. The 30-acre resort, which opened in 2003, resembles an aged California Craftsman retreat, an architectural style that was popular at the time Laguna Beach was just getting settled. Many of the craftsman-style rooms feature ocean view accommodations, and the bathrooms feel like mini spas with luxurious amenities, candles, and oversized tubs. There is a 20,000 square-foot spa, two restaurants overlooking the water, privileges to local golf courses, and three swimming pools. The service is simply superb. *Info:* www.montagelagunabeach.com. Tel. 949/ 715-6000. Laguna Beach. 30801 South Coast Highway. 262 rooms and suites.

The Ritz-Carlton, Laguna Niguel $$$

Although the name says "Laguna Niguel," this Ritz-Carlton is actually located along a pristine coastal bluff in Dana Point. A recent renovation has resulted in a less formal, more inviting ambiance. The public spaces have always been

spectacular, and the guest rooms are just stunning with colors reflective of its seaside setting. The resort's signature restaurant and bar both overlook the ocean. You'll also find a spa, swimming pool, tennis courts, an adjacent golf course, and activities for the kids. *Info:* www.ritzcarlton.com/resorts/laguna_niguel. Tel. 949/ 240-2000. Dana Point. One Ritz-Carlton Drive. 393 rooms and suites.

Surf and Sand Resort $$$

The Surf and Sand Resort was doing the whole mid-century thing long before anyone else. That's because this boxy, multi-story hideaway was built in the 1950s when mid-century was in vogue – a style that is now back and more popular than ever. The Surf and Sand is plush, but not pretentious. Five towers house the various rooms and suites, which are light and airy – just like a stay at the shore should be. Splashes, the resort's intimate restaurant, is aptly named because of its location to the surf. There's a pool and spa plus easy access to the beach. *Info:* www.surfandsandresort.com. Tel. 949/497-4477. Laguna Beach. 1555 South Coast Highway. 165 rooms and suites.

Disneyland Resort Hotels $$

If you're building your itinerary around time spent at Disneyland Resort, then you should seriously consider staying at one of the three resorts located at the park for convenience. All three hotels have dining options, swimming pools, and are within walking distance to the main admission gate. There are three Disney properties to consider: **Disney's Grand Californian** (1600 South Disney Drive. Tel. 714/635-2300. 745 rooms and suites) can be accessed from both Downtown Disney and Disney's California Adventure. The original **Disneyland Hotel** (1150 Magic Way. Tel. 714/778-6600. 990 rooms and suites) is adjacent to Downtown Disney with rooms divided among three hi-rise towers. **Disney's Paradise Pier** (1717 South Disney Drive, Tel. 714/999-0990. 489 rooms and suites) is located the furthest from the entrance gate. Hotel packages typically include passes to both Disneyland and Disney's California Adventure. *Info:* www.disneylandresort.com.

Hilton Waterfront Beach Resort $$

Located across from the beach and overlooking a pristine stretch of sandy coastline, the linear Hilton Waterfront Resort houses rooms with either full or partial ocean views and private balconies. The beach is just across Pacific Coast Highway, which makes it convenient for daytime tanning and nighttime bonfires (the hotel will provide marshmallows and firewood for an additional charge). *Info:* www.waterfrontresort.com. Tel. 714/845-8000. Huntington Beach. 21100 Pacific Coast Highway. 290 guest rooms and suites.

Orange County

Hyatt Regency Huntington Beach Resort & Spa $$
Beautiful Spanish architecture coupled with meandering pathways and breathtaking ocean views make for a relaxing and pampered escape at this luxe, full-serive Hyatt resort. The rooms are very spacious and nicely appointed with private balconies and a view (take your pick: ocean, pool or courtyard). Plus there is a full-service spa, three restaurants, and a lagoon-style swimming. There is a bridge positioned over Pacific Coast Highway that connects the resort to the beach. *Info:* www.huntingtonbeach.hyatt.com. Tel. 714/698-1234. Huntington Beach. 21500 Pacific Coast Highway. 517 rooms and suites.

The Island Hotel $$
This former Four Seasons Hotel picked up where its predecessor left off. Tasteful and posh, the hotel's name refers to its stylish location adjacent to Fashion Island – OC's premiere shopping destination. Nearby is Corona del Mar, Laguna Beach and Balboa Island, all charming destinations. The rooms are ample in size, especially some of the corner rooms, which are billed as Executive Suites. You'll also find a 4,000 square-foot spa; a swimming pool, a pair of restaurants, and

The OCeanfront Alliance

Many of the coastal hotels I recommend for Orange County are part of an alliance called **The OCeanfront**, which promotes the best of the coastal resorts. With just a click of the mouse, you can access information about the properties, including links for online reservations. You can further explore the four beach communities that comprise The OCeanfront, as well as learn about the area's shopping and golf options. *Info:* www.theOCeanfrontCA.com.

lighted tennis courts. If you like to shop, this is the place to stay. *Info:* www.theislandhotel.com. Tel. 949/759-0808. Newport Beach. 690 Newport Center Drive. 295 guest rooms and suites.

Laguna Cliffs Marriott Resort & Spa $$

This resort is ideal for parents traveling with children because it's very luxurious and family friendly. Perched high on the cliffs above Dana Point Harbor, the views are spectacular once the fog lifts. Rooms, which are very nicely appointed and include a small balcony, are located in horseshoe-shaped wings that encircle the resort's pair of ocean view swimming pools. The hotel offers two restaurants, including Vue with its patio setting and savory menu, as well as a lounge just off the lobby. The spa is spectacular, too. *Info:* www.lagunacliffs.com. Tel. 949/661-5000. Dana Point. 25135 Park Lantern. 376 rooms and suites.

Blue Lantern Inn $

This charming three-story bed and breakfast, which teeters high above a coastal bluff, boasts commanding views of the harbor. The handful of rooms all come with a sitting area, fireplace, refrigerator stocked with complimentary soft drinks, and high speed Internet access. A few rooms have private decks with envious views. The rate includes a full breakfast and afternoon wine. *Info:* www.bluelanterninn.com. Tel. 949/661-1304. Dana Point. 34343 Street of the Blue Lantern. 29 rooms and suites.

Casa Laguna Inn $

Terraced on a hillside is this 1930s Mediterranean-style bed and breakfast with its landmark bell tower. The gardens are blessed with blooming bougainvillea and swaying palms and feature a lovely swimming pool. The rooms range in size, from small and intimate to rather roomy, some have fireplaces and others wood floors. Full breakfast and evening wine included. Victoria Beach, known for its white sands and famous residents, is located on the other side of Coast Highway and down the hill. *Info:* www.casalaguna.com. Tel. 949/494-2996. Laguna Beach. 2510 South Coast Highway. 20 rooms and suites.

Crystal Cove Beach Cottages $

Located in the heart of Crystal Cove State Park is a cluster of recently restored, beachfront clapboard cottages. Originally built in the 1920s and first developed as a South Seas movie set, this charming and rustic enclave includes both individual and dorm-style cottages. Reservations are taken throughout the year, but there is a long and growing waiting list. There are two very casual restaurants for added convenience. If you can't finagle a reservation at Crystal Cove Beach Cottages, try taking a tour of the Historic District the second Saturday of the month from January to November. *Info:* www.crystalcovebeachcottages.org. Tel. 800/444-7275. Crystal Cove State Park. Laguna Beach. 11 cottages and 3 dorm-style cottage buildings.

Orange County

Fairmont Newport Beach $

Located not far from the John Wayne Airport, this Fairmont Hotel has only two things going for it: luxury and location. What else do you need? You're near the 405 Freeway, which can take you up towards Los Angeles or south towards San Diego, plus South Coast Plaza and Fashion Island are just minutes away. The beach is also fairly close, and Disneyland is just a bit to the north. The rooms are capsules of luxury, the public spaces spectacular, and the restaurant Bambu has been receiving glowing reviews. *Info:* www.fairmont.com. Tel. 949/476-2001. Newport Beach. 4500 MacArthur Blvd. 440 rooms and suites.

BEST EATS
Blue Coral Seafood & Spirits $$$

Washed ashore at Newport Beach's tony Fashion Island, Blue Coral Seafood & Spirits pays homage to the wonders of the sea. The décor is imaginative, from the illuminated coral glass sculpture to the faux water droplet chandelier. The seasonal menu is also artistic with entrees categorized by "fins," "shells," and "land and air." The wine list features 60 selections by the glass, but it's the "wall of vodka," a display of varying shaped bottles illuminated under electric blue lighting, that seems to turn heads. *Info:*

www.bluecoralseafood.com. Tel. 949/856-2583. Newport Beach/ Fashion Island. 451 Newport Center Drive.

La Fondue $$$

Fondue, along with Tupperware and shag carpeting, may have peaked in the late 1960s but these melting pot meals are making a comeback. While meat and seafood are among the entrée choices, cheese and chocolate fondue still ranks the highest among devoted dippers. The wine list is nice, and the setting is extremely romantic. The restaurant is located near the historic mission. *Info:* www.lafondue.com. Tel. 949/240-0330. San Juan Capistrano. 31761 Camino Capistrano.

Le Quai $$$

Located on the Rhine Channel in Newport Beach's Cannery Village, Le Quai boasts a snug but stylish space with wine lockers lining the lobby and tables and mirrors positioned to make the most of the waterfront view. The menu is a work of art both in terms of taste and presentation. Favorites include lobster bisque, ahi tuna, and a tender Jidori chicken. The wine list is long and deserving of more than just a leisurely glance. *Info:* Tel. 949/673-9463. Newport Beach. 2816 Lafayette Avenue.

Splashes $$$

Located just a few feet above the ocean on the ground level of the

Surf and Sand Hotel is the very intimate Splashes restaurant. Every table offers an ocean view, whether you're dining indoors or out on the terrace. The menu changes daily in order to offer the freshest fish and meat, but staples include halibut, John Dory and veal. The wine list is quite impressive, and there is a full bar too. Splashes Lounge, located just below the restaurant, has a more casual, less expensive menu with the same views. *Info:* www.surfandsandresort.com. Tel. 949/376-2779. Laguna Beach. 1555 South Coast Highway.

The Loft $$$

Housed on the fourth floor of the Montage Resort & Spa, The Loft offers a splendid dining experience coupled with fabulous

panoramic ocean views. The seasonal American menu is served for breakfast, lunch and dinner. Items range from gourmet sandwiches and soups for lunch to fresh seafood dishes and cuts of beef for dinner. The children's menu features all the classic favorites for under $6 and includes a drink and dessert. *Info:* www.montagelagunabeach.com. Tel. 949/715-6420. Laguna Beach. 30801 South Coast Highway.

Orange County

Beach House $$

The Beach House occupies the former home of Hollywood film star Slim Summerville, whose acting credits include *Jessse James* and *Rebecca of Sunnybrook Farm*. The inside dining room resembles an elegant green house with lots of glass, but I'd gladly wait for a table on the small, beachfront terrace. The menu puts an emphasis on seafood, but there are plenty of non-seafood items to choose from. *Info:* www.thebeachhouse.com. Tel. 949/494-9707. Laguna Beach. 619 Sleepy Hollow Lane.

Daimons $$

Daimons, located on a lonely stretch of Pacific Coast Highway in Huntington Beach, is a lively destination that feels like a non-stop house party no matter what hour of the evening you happen to wander in. Daimons is a sensory experience that's loud, informal, and a great place to enjoy sushi and teppan specialties. There's a DJ spinning great music nightly and a sushi chef that's been known to take a beer break with guests. *Info:* Tel. 562/592-4852. Huntington Beach. 16232 Pacific Coast Highway.

230 Forest Avenue $$

230 Forest Avenue is equal parts art gallery, eatery and lounge with a contagious energy that draws people to its threshold. The space, located a block from the beach, is intimate with both indoor and outdoor seating along Forest Avenue. The emphasis is on fresh seafood and dry aged steaks, but there is also an assortment of salads, sandwiches, pasta and appetizers as well.

Orange County

Great place to go for just drinks and nibbles – just ask the locals who pour in here daily. *Info:* www.230forestavenue.com. Tel. 949/494-2545. Laguna Beach. 230 Forest Avenue.

Café Zinc & Market $
Streamline dining is done at this popular outdoor café where actresses Julia Louis-Dreyfuss, Bette Midler and Heather Locklear have been spotted on occasion. The menu has a healthy bent to it, so you can feel good about what you're eating. You'll find egg dishes, scones, soup, salads and sandwiches available. Most of the breads arrive from either La Brea Bakery or Il Forniao. *Info:* www.cafezinc.com. Tel. 949/494-6302. Laguna Beach. 350 Ocean Avenue.

The Crab Cooker $
You can't miss The Crab Cooker's red shack along busy Newport Boulevard. The neon sign has been directing folks to the restaurant for more than half a century, and the long lines are proof of its popularity. Fresh fish is delivered on paper plates and, for less than $20 per person, you can order oysters on the half shell, crab cakes, or king crab claws. Wine and beer available. *Info:* www.crabcooker.com. Tel. 949/673-0100. Newport Beach. 2200 Newport Boulevard.

Taco Surf $
Designed to look like a seaside Mexican cantina, Taco Surf is popular among the locals. The restaurant has great salsa and fresh guacamole, along with a list of tacos, burritos, fish, quesadillas and tostadas. Beer, wine and margaritas are available, too. If you want to save even more money, come during the week

Dining at Disney

If you're staying at the Disneyland Resort, there are many places to dine right on the premises. Avoid the restaurants inside either park, which are mostly expensive, fast food stops; instead, head to **Downtown Disney**. My recommendations include **La Brea Bakery, Catal Restaurant** or **Naples Ristorante e Pizzeria** (they have a small café next door that is great for a quick bite – **Napolini**). For a truly elegant meal, make a reservation at the **Napa Rose** located inside Disney's Grand Californian Hotel.

between 3pm-6pm when tacos are just $1. *Info:* www.tacosurf.com. Tel. 949/661-5754. Dana Point. 34195 Pacific Coast Highway.

CATALINA ISLAND

Note: You'll secure the best nightly rate on Catalina Island if you arrive midweek during the winter months.

Inn on Mt. Ada $$$
If you're planning on doing an overnight trip to Catalina Island, my first hotel choice would be the Inn on Mt. Ada, a luxurious, five room bed and breakfast inn and the former home of chewing gum magnate William Wrigley. Included in the nightly rate is the use of a golf cart to putt around the island, a full breakfast, a deli lunch and snack privileges throughout the day. *Info:* www.innonmtada.com. Tel. 310/510-2030.

Snug Harbor Inn $$
Six rooms, stylish accommodations, and harbor views. *Info:* www.snugharbor-inn.com. Tel. 888/394-7684.

Villa Portofino $
Overlooks the harbor. *Info:* www.hotelvillaportofino.com. Tel. 310/510-0555).

SANTA BARBARA

BEST SLEEPS
Four Seasons Biltmore $$$
This 1927 Spanish Colonial resort sits on 21 prime acres of oceanfront property and offers extremely luxurious accommodations. The amenities include guests a private beach club where an oceanside swimming pool and white-sand beach is located. There are two health clubs on the premises, fine dining, tennis courts and croquet. The spa is an oasis of luxury with a menu of very expensive treatments. What sets this hotel apart from its

competitors is the level of service provided by the staff. *Info:* www.fourseasons.com/santabarbara. Tel. 805/961-2261. Montecito. 1260 Channel Drive. 181 rooms, suites and cottages.

Fess Parker's Wine Country Inn & Spa Vigne $$

If you plan on spending most of your time exploring the wine trails in the Santa Ynez Valley, then you should consider staying at Fess Parker's inn. The rooms are nicely appointed and each stay includes a full American breakfast, and wine tasting for two at Fess Parker's nearby winery. The hotel features a spa and The Wine Cask, a favorite Santa Barbara restaurant now with a second location inside the hotel. You can also walk to some other nearby restaurants in Los Olivos, and you're also close to the Danish town of Solvang. *Info:* www.fessparker.com. Tel. 805/ 688-7788. Los Olivos. 2860 Grand Avenue. 21 rooms and suites.

Fess Parker Double Tree Resort $$

Fess Parker — of Davey Crockett fame — also owns this sprawling full-service resort. Situated across from the beach, guests enjoy a number of amenities including an outdoor swimming pool, exercise room, tennis courts, a full-service spa, a basketball court, and putting green with bike and skate rentals available on the premises. The rooms are very comfortable and nicely appointed, and each has its own patio or balcony with views of the ocean, mountains, swimming pool or courtyard. *Info:* www.fpdtr.com. Tel. 805/564-4333. Beach. 633 E. Cabrillo Boulevard. 360 rooms and suites.

Harbor View Inn $$

This small, luxury inn is inviting from the moment you step into the lobby, where a fleet of French doors are propped open to reveal cool ocean breezes. Overlooking the beach and Stearns Wharf, the two-story hotel has a lovely landscape of tropical gardens, stone paths and ornate fountains. Most of the contemporary rooms have patios overlooking the beach or pool (request one of these when making a reservation). *Info:* www.harborviewinnsb.com. Tel. 805/ 962-6436. Beach. 28 West Cabrillo Boulevard. 102 rooms and suites.

Simpson House Inn $$

This tops my list of absolute favorite places to stay. Guests are housed in the main Victorian mansion, the original 1878 barn, or one of the freestanding garden cottages. A lavish breakfast and equally lavish evening buffet is presented daily. The grounds are

abloom with wisteria and fragrant flora punctuated with trickling fountains. Everything is included in the nightly room rate, and you can walk to all the shops and restaurants along State Street. *Info:* www.simpsonhouseinn.com. Tel. 805/963-7067. Downtown. 121 East Arrellaga Street. 15 rooms, suites and cottages.

Tiffany Country House $$
You'll enjoy the time you spend at this three-story Victorian mansion. The common rooms, located on the first floor, include an antique-filled living room and dining room where morning coffee is enjoyed. The second floor contains six individually-appointed guest rooms each with private baths. The loft-like Penthouse Suite, with its own entrance, occupies the entire third floor and includes a living room, fireplace and whirlpool tub. Each stay includes a full breakfast enjoyed on the backyard verandah, as well as evening wine and cheese. *Info:* www.countryhouseinns.com. Tel. 805/963-2283. Downtown. 1323 De La Vina Street. 7 rooms.

The Upham Hotel $$
This is Santa Barbara's oldest and continuously operating hotel having opened in 1871. Situated a block from State Street, the inn combines the attentive service of a bed and breakfast with many amenities expected from a top-notch hotel. You can choose to sleep in the main inn, one of the garden cottages or the carriage house. A complimentary buffet breakfast and afternoon wine and cheese are included in the room rate. Louie's Restaurant, a popular Santa Barbara bistro, is located on the premises. *Info:* www.uphamhotel.com. Tel. 805/962-0876. Downtown. 1404 De La Vina Street. 49 rooms, suites and cottages.

Cheshire Cat Inn $
The Cheshire Cat is actually two 19th-century Victorian homes

joined together by a courtyard, where breakfast is served each morning and guests gather in the afternoon to sample local wines and enjoy hors d'oeuvres. A trio of 1930s, self-contained bungalows across the street is ideal for adults traveling with children. The Coach House, located behind the main homes, also features additional and very private rooms. The inn is just above downtown and within easy walking distance to the shops and restaurants, or head the other direction and stroll to the Mission. Free wireless Internet. *Info:* www.cheshirecat.com. Tel. 805/569-1610. Downtown. 36 West Valerio Street. 17 rooms and suites.

Franciscan Inn $

Located on a quiet street just a block from the beach, the original 1920s Spanish-style ranch home has been incorporated into this red-tiled roof complex. Room designs and amenities vary to include cast iron beds, wood beam ceilings, wet bars, fireplaces and, in some cases, kitchens. Mornings begin with an array of complimentary pastries and coffee with refreshments offered in the afternoon. There is a heated swimming pool and spa as well. *Info:* www.franciscaninn.com. Tel. 805/963-8845. Beach. 109 Bath Street. 53 rooms and suites.

Hotel Virginia - Holiday Inn Express $

The building that houses the Holiday Inn Express was built between 1916 and 1925 and opened as Hotel Virginia. Because of its historic significance, the hotel, which is located in the heart of downtown Santa Barbara just blocks from the beach, is not like your typical Holiday Inn. The lobby has a lovely vintage tile fountain, and the rooms have exposed brick walls and large, picture windows. A complimentary buffet breakfast is served each morning and free high-speed Internet access is available. *Info:* www.hotelvirginia.com. Tel. 805/963-9757. Downtown. 17 West Hayley St. 61 rooms.

BEST EATS
Bouchon $$$

Touted as one of Santa Barbara's best fine dining restaurants, Bouchon offers wine country cuisine and serves fabulous vintages reflective of the region. Bouchon offers a seasonal menu with some very creative twists on traditional dishes: spiny lobster pot pie, escargot in puff pastry, and grilled, boneless Cornish game hen. *Info:* www.bouchonsantabarbara.com. Tel. 805/730-1166. Downtown. 9 West Victoria Street.

Café Buenos Aires $$

This charming restaurant, located across the street from the historic Arlington Theater, offers an array of Argentine-inspired cuisine. The menu, call it Latin American fusion, features a selection of empanadas and other regional dishes, including a Latin-style Shepard's Pie with layers of ground sirloin, olives, raisins and basil. The outdoor patio, which features a cabana-style awning that can retract, offers the best tables. *Info:* www.cafebuenosaires.com. Tel. 805/963-0242. Downtown. 1316 State Street.

Chad's on Chapala $$

Owner and chef Chad Stevens' signature restaurant is located in a charming 19th-century Victorian home that faces the backside of the Paseo Nuevo shopping center. Regional American dishes take precedence with a selection of fresh pastas, seafood, beef and chops. You'll also find a menu of seasonal specials as well as a wine and martini list. Stop in for happy hour Monday-Saturday from 4:30-6:30pm when half-priced drinks and appetizers are served on the heated outdoor patio. *Info:* www.chads.biz. Tel. 805/568-1876. Downtown. 625 Chapala Street.

Best Waterfront Eats

These are Santa Barbara's best waterfront restaurants:
• **Shoreline Beach Café**, 801 Shoreline Drive. Tel. 805/568-0064
• **Harbor Restaurant**, Stearns Wharf. Tel. 805/963-3311
• **Longboard's**, Stearns Wharf. Tel. 805/963-3311
• **Endless Summer Bar-Café**, 113 Harbor Way. Tel. 805/564-1200
• **Brophy Bros. Restaurant & Clam Bar**, 119 Harbor Way. Tel. 805/966-4418

Los Olivos Café $$

Located in the heart of Santa Barbara's Wine County, Los Olivos Café may feel a bit familiar to movie buffs. Featured in the film

Santa
Barbara

Sideways (where Jack and Miles meet Maya and Stephanie for dinner), the restaurant has been a mainstay along Grand Avenue for more than a decade. Serving reasonably priced California cuisine with a Mediterranean twist, the restaurant offers indoor and patio seating as well as 20 stools at the wine bar. Entrees include gourmet sandwiches, salads and pasta, plus a few specials. *Info:* www.losolivoscafe.com. Tel. 805/688-7265. Los Olivos. 2879 Grand Avenue.

Opal Restaurant and Bar $$
Located next to the historic Arlington Theater, Opal Restaurant and Bar resembles a Parisian bistro with its large picture windows, black and white tile floors, and a scattering of tables. You'll dine on an eclectic menu of salads, pizza, pasta, poultry and seafood both for lunch and dinner. There are some 300 wines with more than 40 offered by the glass. *Info:* www.opalrestaurantandbar.com. Tel. 805/966-9676. Downtown. 1327 State Street.

Paradise Café $$
The vintage 1915 brick and stucco building that houses the Paradise Café has a very Art Deco feel to it. The restaurant has a delightful bar and offers outdoor dining. This little bistro is open for lunch and dinner plus serves brunch on Sunday morning. You'll find a selection of grilled steaks and fish, sandwiches, salads and the restaurant's famed Paradise Burger. *Info:* www.paradisecafe.com. Tel. 805/962-4416. Downtown. 702 Anacapa Street.

Wine Cask $$
Located in the historic El Paseo, the interior of the Wine Cask features a dining room with a hand-painted beam ceiling and a baronial fireplace, as well as a lovely and secluded courtyard. The bistro-style menu includes gourmet sandwiches and pastas for lunch and foie gras, duck lobster and tuna tartar for dinner. The restaurant also offers a tasting menu, as well as an extensive wine list. **Intermezzo**, the restaurant's adjacent wine bar, offers light fare and a lovely setting. *Info:* www.winecask.com. Tel. 805/966-9463. Downtown. 813 Anacapa Street.

Aldo's Italian Restaurant $
Housed in an 1857 adobe-style building, Aldo's prepares consistently good, classic Italian food. A handful of tables are located on the small, fountain courtyard, which fronts State Street. The lunch and dinner menu features a number of pasta dishes, veal, pizza, sandwiches – all served in ample-sized portions. *Info:* www.sbaldos.com. Tel. 805/963-6687. Downtown. 1031 State Street.

Barcliff & Bair $
This charming sidewalk café is open for breakfast and lunch. On the menu you'll find an assortment of sandwiches and soups coupled with daily specials and, on occasion, afternoon tea is offered with all the accouterments. A recent expansion has resulted in additional indoor seating, but the best tables are those along the sidewalk. *Info:* Tel. 805/965-5742. Downtown. 1112 State Street.

La Super Rica $
You can't write about Santa Barbara's best restaurants without giving a nod to this hole-in-the-wall Mexican restaurant. The late Julia Child was a regular, so you know the food has to be good. The

Picnic Lunch Delight!

Santa Barbara

If you're heading to the beach, the wine country or even the Santa Barbara Zoo (the zoo has picnic areas and allows outside food to be brought in), you might want to pack your picnic hamper with lunch from one of these delicatessens.

• **Italian and Greek Deli**, 636 State Street. Tel. 805/962-6815. Classic deli with huge submarine sandwiches and case full of fresh salads.

• **Pierre LaFond**, 11 West De la Guerra in the Paseo Nuevo Shopping Center. Tel. 805/966-5290. Gourmet sandwiches, wraps and salads.

• **Los Olivos Grocery**, 2621 Highway 154 in Santa Ynez. Tel. 805/688-5115. Located n the heart of wine country and offering an array of sandwiches and salads.

• **Trader Joe's,** 29 South Milpas Street. Tel. 805/564-7878. Inexpensive, gourmet market with pre-packaged meats and cheeses, as well as salads and desserts.

menu offers authentic tacos with no-fuss fillings of marinated pork or chicken. Gorditas and homemade tamales are just some of the specialties. Lines are long and you'll have to hunt for a table on the ramshackle, covered patio. *Info:* Tel. 805/963-4940. East of Downtown. 622 North Milpas Street. Cash only.

Pascucci's $
Long lines are the sign of a good restaurant, and the queues at Pascucci's are never ending. The restaurant offers limited patio dining, a small section of curtained booths with additional booths and tables located in the restaurant's indoor "Italian piazza." Everything that's turned out by the kitchen staff is excellent, from the grilled sandwiches and salads to plate after plate of pasta. There is a selection of local wines, a few taps of beer, and a children's menu. *Info:* www.pascuccirestaurant.com. Tel. 805/963-8123. Downtown. 729 State Street.

Shang Hais $
You're not likely to find many visitors dining at Shang Hais. That's because this Chinese restaurant, where director Robert Zemeckis hosted a post-Oscar party to celebrate his award-winning film *Forrest Gump*, is a favorite among locals. The menu includes all the traditional favorites, as well as many vegetarian dishes, such as Kung Pao Beef and Sweet and Sour Chicken, both made with tofu instead of meat. *Info:* Tel. 805/962-7833. East of Downtown. 830 North Milpas Street.

PALM SPRINGS

BEST SLEEPS
Visiting Palm Springs is a bit of a catch-22. The best time to visit is from late fall to early spring, when all the attractions are open and operating. Of course, you can also expect to pay premium rates at all the hotels and resorts. If you want to save money and can take the triple-digit heat, then visit between mid-June to mid-September when you'll find the rates at hotels and golf courses at their lowest.

The Willows Historic Palm Springs Inn $$-$$$

This airy 1924 hilltop villa, once the private oasis of Marion Davis, is one of the area's most magnificent inns. The two-story Italian manse features a small collection of rooms, curved archways, wrought-iron balustrades and vaulted ceilings with hardwood and slate flooring throughout. The dining room, where complimentary breakfast is served, is carved into the desert rock and features a two-story cascading waterfall. There is a small swimming  pool on the premises, and at the end of the street are lots of shops and restaurants along Palm Canyon Drive. Afternoon wine and cheese served daily. *Info:* www.thewillowspalmsprings.com. Tel. 760/320-0771. Palm Springs. 412 West Tahquitz Canyon Way. 8 rooms and suites.

Smoke Tree Ranch $$

There is more beneath the surface of Palm Springs than swimming pools and the latest spa treatment. For a completely different desert experience, book a room at the rustic Smoke Tree Ranch. The 1930s-era compound includes an enclave of one and two-bedroom cottages, some 400 mostly undeveloped acres, an extremely private location, spa treatments and stables where you can saddle up for a horseback ride. The ranch also offers full meal plans. *Info:* www.smoketreeranch.com. Tel. 760/327-1221. Palm Springs. 1850 Smoke Tree Lane. 57 cottages.

Korakia Pensione $$

The inn, located in the heart of Palm Springs and within walking distance to shops and restaurants, is actually the marriage of two homes joined together by a common breezeway. One home, built in 1924 and inspired by the architecture of Tangier, belonged to Scottish Painter Gordon Coutts and the other, a 1934 Mediterranean-style villa, to actor J. Carol Nash. Set against the spectacular San Jacinto Mountains on nearly two acres, each room is full of luxurious appointments. Breakfast is served en suite or at a table near the pool. *Info:* www.korakia.com. Tel. 760/864-6411. Palm Springs. 257 South Patencios. 22 rooms and suites.

La Quinta Resort & Club $$

Designed in true Spanish tradition, accommodations at La Quinta are positioned around a series of courtyards. Built in 1925, the resort inspired Irving Berlin to write the classic tune *White Christmas* after spending a sweltering December at the resort. La Quinta, though large with 23 tennis courts, 42 pools, 52 hot tubs, and five restaurants, manages to feel like a very intimate, exclusive resort. There are suites, spa suites and the original freestanding casitas. Spa La Quinta is a wonderful addition to this vintage resort with many of the treatments borrowed from the area's Native American ancestors. *Info:* www.laquintaresort.com. Tel. 760/564-4111. La Quinta. 49-499 Eisenhower Drive. 800 suites and casitas.

Miramonte Resort & Spa $$

Built to resemble a Tuscan-style villa, the attention paid to the

architectural detail is evident with hand-laid stonework, wrought-iron accents and thick columns supporting mezzanines. Rooms, which feature private terraces and high-speed Internet access, are housed in one of 14 freestanding villas. Recreation includes a fitness center, three outdoor cabana-lined pools, a championship golf course and tennis. *Info:* www.miramonteresort.com. Tel. 760/341-2200. 76-477 Highway 111. 215 rooms and suites.

Renaissance Esmeralda Resort and Spa $$

Set against the Santa Rosa Mountains is this Mediterranean-style resort with its eight-story atrium lobby and stunning collection of art. Rooms are spacious and nicely appointed, and kids enjoy free room service with an adult paid entrée – an added and money-saving convenience. Surrounded by 36 holes of championship golf courses designed by Ted Robinson, you can take advantage of a pair of fitness centers, tennis courts, and swimming pools including one with a sandy beach for kids. There is a renowned spa plus four restaurants and upscale shops. *Info:* www.renaissanceesmeralda.com. Tel. 760/773-4444. Indian Wells. 44-400 Indian Wells Lane. 560 rooms and suites.

Villa Royale Inn $$

This delightful inn features a collection of rooms concealing a series of inner courtyards with private entrances, paver tiles, wood-beam ceilings, and four-poster beds. There are two swimming pools and in-room spa treatments, plus a full breakfast included with the rate. The inn is home to Europa Restaurant, where you can conveniently slip inside the intimate bar for a drink or enjoy dinner overlooking the pool. *Info:* www.villaroyale.com. Tel. 760/327-2314. Palm Springs. 1620 Indian Trail. 33 rooms and suites.

Palm Springs

Orbit In $

Putting the groove back in groovy is Orbit In, a hip and happening mid-century retreat. Located in the Tennis Club District, just blocks off Palm Canyon Drive, the hotel prides itself on its fun and functional furnishings. The nightly rate includes a continental breakfast served poolside and a menu of in-room spa treatments that must be booked before arrival. *Info:* www.orbitin.com. Tel. 760/ 323-3585. Palm Springs. 562 West Arenas. 9 studio rooms.

BEST EATS

Agusta at Plaza Roberge $$$

This two-story restaurant is opulent and stunning. A winding staircase leads to the loft-style dining area above, which verlooks the exhibition kitchen and main dining room below. The menu is a creative force of sophisticated offerings, from lamb and duck to Chilean

Sleep Like a Star!

If you prefer to sleep like a star in Palm Springs, consider renting one of these private homes:

• **Phillips Estate**, located in an exclusive area with panoramic views, once belonged to John Phillips of the Mamas and the Papas.

• **Twin Palms Sinatra Estate**, located in the Movie Colony and featuring a piano-shaped swimming pool, was the home of ol' Blue Eyes.

• **Sandacre**, an elegant five-bedroom Spanish hacienda, was one of the homes where Joe DiMaggio and Marilyn Monroe lived during their brief marriage.

Info: Time & Place Homes, Tel. 866/244-1800.

sea bass and spicy grilled shrimp. *Info:* www.plazaroberge.com. Tel. 760/779-9200. Palm Desert. 73-951 El Paseo.

The Chop House $$$

A sanctuary for carnivores, this lovely dinner-only restaurant features an array of USDA prime-aged steaks and chops. All meats are butchered in-house, grilled longer and at lower temperatures, and then brought to your table ultra-tender. The interiors are plush with rock walls, rolling columns of curved brick, warm wood paneling and a dramatic two-story atrium. *Info:* www.chophousepalmdesert. Tel. 760/779-9888. Palm Desert. 74-040 Highway 111.

Cuistot $$$

The French chef/owner of this enchanting restaurant has worked at many renowned resorts. His menu is like a culinary tour of France. A handful of entrees range from rabbit to stuffed quail, and the wine list seems never ending. *Info:* www.cuistotrestaurant.com. Tel. 760/340-1000. Palm Desert. 72-595 El Paseo.

Le Vallauris $$$

Located off Palm Canyon Drive and housed in an historic home, this is an elegant retreat with excellent service. The daily menu is presented on a hand-written board and includes a selection of French fare, from traditional appetizers such as foie gras to entrees made with lamb, veal, beef or lobster all dressed in unique sauces. The setting is refined with tapestries and antiques, and the outdoor terrace is extremely romantic. *Info:* www.levallauris.com. Tel. 760/325-5059. Palm Springs. 385 West Tahquitz Canyon Way.

Wally's Desert Turtle $$$

Opened for nearly three decades, Wally's Desert Turtle enjoys a loyal following. You'll dine under a beveled mirrored ceiling in an opulent room filled with Peruvian artifacts and hand-painted murals. The menu offers hors d'oeuvres, seafood and beef entrees, fish and shellfish, and a list of creative pastas. The wine list is extensive with many vintages hailing from California vineyards. *Info:* www.wallys-desert-turtle.com. Tel. 760/568-9321. Rancho Mirage. 71-775 Highway 111.

Café Des Beaux-Arts $$

A touch of Paris is found beneath the desert sun at this informal and unassuming café. French onion soup, stuffed lobster ravioli and steak au poivre create a formal touch for the palate. In addition to lunch and dinner, Café Des Beaux Arts is also open for breakfast and serves traditional meals and crepes. The wine list features mostly French varieties. *Info:* www.cafedesbeauxarts.com. Tel. 760/346-0669. Palm Desert. 73-640 El Paseo.

Vicky's of Santa Fe $$

Its high ceilings, vivid color scheme and Mission-style furniture provides the southwestern setting needed for this desert adobe. The menu, however, is more traditional with a selection of rotisserie chicken, 16-ounce Nebraska corn-fed beef and chops, and such tried and true dishes as liver and onions and chicken pot pie. A nice selection of wine and live piano music on  selective evenings makes Vicky's a standout. *Info:* www.vickysofsantafe.com. Tel. 760/345-9770. Indian Wells. 45-100 Club Drive.

Blue Coyote Grill $

With a great ambiance and food at the right price, Blue Coyote Grill makes for a delightful dining experience. The entrees offer true southwestern flavors and Yucatan-style specialties. The most popular tables during double-digit weather are those on the outdoor patio where red tile floors, pockets of little gardens and twinkle lights make the experience even more enjoyable. Blue Coyote Grill's margaritas are legendary. *Info:* www.bluecoyote-grill.com. Tel. 760/327-1196. Palm Springs. 445 N. Palm Canyon Drive.

Dale's Lost Highway $

Serving distinctively American food inspired by diners found along our nation's highways, the Route 66 menu at this roadhouse cafe is basic, straightforward and delicious. It's all about comfort food, from the barbecue selections to the Tex-Mex offerings. Ice-cold margaritas and pitchers of beer make for a casual lunch or dinner. The homemade desserts are designed to serve four. *Info:* www.daleslosthighway.com. Tel. 760/327-2005. Palm Springs.125 E. Tahquitz

Las Casuealas Terraza $
This classic restaurant along Palm Canyon Drive offers a long list of Mexican favorites and salt-rimmed margaritas. The adobe setting conceals a Spanish-style village with dining inside or on the always-crowded outdoor patio where nightly entertainment creates a packed house. *Info:* www.lascasuelas.com. Tel. 760/325-2794. Palm Springs. 222 South Palm Canyon Drive.

Take Your Pick!

Not sure what you're in the mood for? Then head to the **River at Rancho Mirage** on Highway 111 at Bob Hope Drive in the city of Rancho Mirage. This lifestyle entertainment has a Borders Books & Music, multiplex cinema, and a variety of well-known and not so well known restaurants, including Babe's Bar-B-Que & Brewery, Fleming's Prime Steakhouse, Maki Maki California Japanese Cuisine, PF Chang's China Bistro, Piero's Acqua Pazza, Cheesecake Factory, and Yard House.

10. BEST ACTIVITIES

This chapter provides an overview of some of Southern California's best vacation activities: **shopping, nightlife,** and year-round **sports and recreation.** You'll discover some fabulous shopping destinations, friendly bars, trendy nightclubs, relaxing places for a spa treatment, and suggestions for enjoying the great outdoors.

LOS ANGELES

BEST SHOPPING

You won't be bored by what Los Angeles has to offer in terms of shopping. There are plenty of malls, but only a few really standout among the crowd. **The Grove** at Third and Fairfax is one of them. It's designed to look like a European square with bubbling fountains and storefronts lining the cobblestone pathways. There is a Nordstrom, Sur La Table, Pottery Barn Kids and much more, plus lots of outdoor dining, a state-of-the-art movie theater and a faux trolley that connects this new destination with an LA landmark – Farmers Market. *Info:* www.thegrovela.com.

It used to be all the trendsetters swarmed Melrose Avenue, which is now so '80s (it's still fun, but looking a little worn). Now hip Angelenos head to the **100 block of Robertson** Avenue on LA's west side. The paparazzi are also camped out along this stretch in hopes of landing the next cover of *US Weekly* with a photo of Paris, Lindsey, Nicole, Jessica and all those Jennifers. The most popular store on this street is **Kitson**. Stars, especially twenty- and thirtysomethings, love to shop here, and it's stocked with lots of fun stuff. Remember those t-shirts "Mrs. Brad Pitt" or "Team Aniston"? That short-lived trend began at Kitson. *Info:* Tel. 310/859-2652. 115 S. Roberston. **The Ivy** *(see LA's Best Eats)* is located less than a block away and is a great pit stop to grab lunch and star gaze.

From designer duds at retail prices to designer duds at close to wholesale prices, it's the **Fashion District** in downtown LA. The general boundaries for the 90-block district are

Shopping Tours

Book a tour of the Fashion District with **Urban Shopping Adventures**. These are custom designed to meet your shopping needs, last about three hours, and include some additional discounts not afforded to the general public. The cost is about $40 per person and well worth it – reservation required. *Info:* Urban Shopping Adventures, Tel. 213/683-9715, www.urbanshoppingadventures.com.

from 7th Street to the north, Santa Monica Freeway to the south, Spring and Main Streets to the west, and San Pedro Street to the east. This is a bargain hunter's paradise with more than 1,000 stores that sell to the general public at heavily discounted prices. Retailers in this area are independent, so you'll find unique items that you're not likely to find at the mall. Shoppers can expect to save 30-70% off retail prices on apparel and accessories for the entire family. On Saturdays, the busiest day of the week for bargain hunters, many wholesale-only stores will sell to the general public. *Info:*  fashiondistrict.com. **Santee Alley** is a pedestrian-only street that has the feel of a bazaar – feel free to bargain here and throughout the Fashion District. Sample Sale Days are held monthly in participating showrooms in the California Market Center, Cooper Design Space, Gerry Building, and The New Mart. These buildings are all located at the intersection of 9th and Los Angeles Streets.

Other great outdoor shopping places in and around Los Angeles include **Montana Avenue** in Santa Monica featuring 150 individual shops, national retailers, and outdoor cafes. *Info:* www.montanaave.com. **Old Town Pasadena** along Colorado Boulevard is home to the Tournament of Roses Parade route. In recent years national retailers have replaced many of the local merchants due to high and demanding rents. Still, this area is historic and filled with shops, restaurants, coffeehouses and bookstores. *Info:*www.oldpasadena.com. **Rodeo Drive** in Beverly Hills remains a classic destination for very high-end designers, though some national retailers have also found their way here. Lots of stars still like to shop along this luxury boulevard and surrounding avenues.

BEST NIGHTLIFE
LA club-goers tend to be fickle. What's hot today may be quickly replaced with something bigger, better and newer tomorrow. A

lot of the buzz focuses around the clubs that cater to the stars, but this often means convincing the bouncer to grant you passage past the velvet rope. Most of the "in" clubs are on LA's westside and Hollywood, and include **LAX** (the club, not the airport), **Hyde Lounge, Cabana Club**, and **Mood.** Rande Gerber (AKA Mr. Cindy Crawford) owns two celebrity-laden hotel bars, **Stone Rose Lounge** in the **Hotel Sofitel** at Beverly and La Cienega across from the Beverly Center, and **The Whiskey Blue** inside the hip **W Hotel** in Westwood.

If you're looking for some inexpensive entertainment, you can't beat the price, setting or sounds at **Los Angeles County Museum of Art** (LACMA)'s **free concert series**:
• Every Friday night from 6-8pm April through Thanksgiving, LACMA presents free jazz concerts on the plaza in the Times Mirror Central Court. These concerts feature leading jazz artists from Southern California.
• In the Leo S. Bing Theater at LACMA enjoy free chamber music concerts year-round every Sunday at 6pm.
• Every Monday from May to September enjoy the Latin Sounds Series outdoors at LACMA.

Downtown Los Angeles is hopping at **The Roof Bar** at The Standard Hotel. Other downtown destinations include the artsy **Mountain Bar**, the **Gallery Bar** where the *Black Dahlia* is said to have had her last drink before her notorious demise, and the swank **Noe Bar** at the Omni Hotel.

West Hollywood's **Santa Monica Boulevard**, between La Cienega and Doheny, is home to LA's thriving gay community. There is bar after bar, club after club along this stretch of road.

Looking for just an average pubcrawl? There are some great British pubs in Santa Monica, including the **Britannia Pub** and **Ye Old King's Head**, both on Santa Monica Boulevard near Third Street. **Old Town Pasadena** along Colorado Avenue has several pubs and lounges, and Pacific Coast Highway in **Malibu** is lined with pubs, bars and upscale lounges, including **Moonshadows** (this is where Mel Gibson was seen before his much publicized arrest), **Duke's**, and **Gladstones** are just a few of the others.

The **Hollywood Bowl**, designed by Frank Lloyd Wright's son, is home to the LA Philharmonic and Hollywood Bowl Orchestra with additional headlining acts rounding out the summer calendar from June-September. There are places to picnic before the concert starts. Tickets start at just $1 per seat. *Info:* www.hollywood.bowl.org. Tel. 323/850-2000. 2301 North Highland Avenue.

LA

The **Greek Theatre**, located in Griffith Park, offers spectacular setting for spring and summer concerts with places to picnic (food must be purchased at the theater). Recent acts have included The White Stripes, Tom Jones, and Chicago, just to name a few. *Info:* www.greektheatrela.com. Tel. 323/665-1927. Griffith Park. 2700 North Vermont Avenue.

If you want the latest scoop on LA's nightlife, check out www.la.com for a complete listing of clubs, pubs, lounges, comedy clubs and everything else that takes place after dark.

BEST SPORTS & RECREATION
No matter what time of year you arrive, there is some professional sport being played on some field, rink, court or track in Los Angeles.

Pro Baseball
There is no better way to spend a summer afternoon or evening than watching a baseball game at Dodger Stadium in Elysian Park near downtown (www.dodgers.com). The regular season runs April-October.

Pro Basketball
Both the **Los Angeles Lakers** (www.lalakers.com) and the **Los Angeles Clippers** (www.losangelesclippers.com) now play at the STAPLES Center in downtown Los Angeles from October-April. Tickets are available at the box office.

Pro & Collegiate Football

Since both the Los Angeles Rams and the Los Angeles Raiders

have made their exodus from Southern California, Angelenos have been without a professional football team. The rumor mill suggests that a team may be swayed to come west, but that remains to be seen. Football junkies can still get their fix from college **PAC 10** teams UCLA and USC from August to December. The **UCLA Bruins** (www.uclabruins.com) play at the Rose Bowl in Pasadena, and the **USC Trojans** (www.usctrojans.cstv.com) play at the Coliseum near downtown Los Angeles.

Pro Hockey

The **Los Angeles Kings** (www.lakings.com) play at the STAPLES Center from November through mid-April.

Horse Racing

Los Angeles offers two tracks where you can watch the ponies run. Generally, the first race beings around 1pm and there are nine races per day. The eighth race is usually the featured race of the day. **Santa Anita Park** (www.santaanita.com), near Pasadena in Arcadia, opens December 26 with the season concluding mid-April. The **Oak Tree** meet runs October and November, and enthusiasts can enjoy morning workouts during race months at no charge. Across town in Inglewood near LAX is **Hollywood Park** (www.hollywoodpark.com), where the race season runs from mid-April to July, and an autumn meet is held mid-November to mid-December.

Pro Soccer

Now that British soccer star David Beckham has joined the team, **The LA Galaxy** (www.lagalaxy.com) may get the respect it deserves. The season runs March through October, and home matches are played at The Home Depot Center in Carson near Long Beach.

Golf

Many of the courses in Los Angeles, such as Bel-Air Country Club and the Riviera Country Club, are strictly members-only destinations. Courses, like the four-course **Griffith Park Golf Club** (www.griffithparkgolfshop.com) and **Heartwell Golf Course** in Long Beach (www.ci.longbeach.ca.us) – where Tiger Woods played as a kid, are open to the public.

Golf Privileges

Many hotels offer their guests **golf privileges** or preferred tee times to local golf courses. Ask your concierge if your hotel offers such a service.

Tennis

Tennis is available at most hotels in the city. If you want to watch a tennis match, UCLA (www.uclabruins.com) hosts many tournaments for free at the campus's L.A. Tennis Center from October through May.

Hiking

There are some rather spectacular places to hike in Los Angeles. The **Santa Monica Mountains** are part of the National Park Service and are located west of Griffith Park in Los Angeles County and to the east of the Oxnard Plain in neighboring Ventura County. There are several roads leading to the area, and your best bet for important information is the visitors' center. There are nearly 600 miles of public trails to be found, and picnicking is also allowed. *Info:* Tel. 818/597-9192. Visitors' center located at 30401 Agoura Road, Agoura Hills.

Malibu Creek State Park in Calabasas is a popular area for filming. *Planet of the Apes* and scenes from *M*A*S*H* were filmed here. There are 15 miles of trails, picturesque Century Lake, and the willow-lined Malibu Creek. *Info:* Tel. 818/880-0367. 1925 Las Virgenes Road, Calabasas.

Biking & Walking

Santa Monica's **paved beach path**, which stretches 22 miles from

Malibu to the north down to Torrance in the south, is the longest of its kind in the world. This is absolutely the best place in LA to walk or bike and, whether you're on it for a mile or the entire length, so much activity unfolds in very little time. *Info:* www.santamonica.com.

Day Spas
Most of the big hotels, and even some of the smaller boutique properties, all have state-of-the-art spas on their premises. Two that offer excellent service and treatments are **The Spa at Le Merigot Hotel** (www.lemerigothotel.com) and the **Be Well Spa** (www.lacenterstudios.com) located on the lot of Los Angeles Center Studios in downtown Los Angeles.

SAN DIEGO

BEST SHOPPING
Horton Plaza is an architectural amalgamation of Spanish, Colonial, Mediterranean, Moorish, Gothic and contemporary styles. This open-air shopping complex is located in the heart of the Gaslamp Quarter in downtown San Diego. There are seven levels twisted around six and a half city blocks anchored by Nordstrom and Macy's; in between there are more than 140 specialty shops, restaurants and services plus a 14-screen cinema. *Info:* www.westfield.com/hortonplaza.

The eclectic **Hillcrest** neighborhood, located a mile north of downtown, is a hip uptown district featuring funky finds, reasonable prices and pedestrian-friendly promenades. This primarily gay neighborhood also features scores of sidewalk cafes and coffeehouses. *Info:* www.hillquest.com.

The colorful marketplace known as **Bazaar Del Mundo** in Old Town resembles a traditional Mexican Mercado with more than 18 shops with many specializing in Mexican folk art, and a handful of restaurants. *Info:* www.bazaardelmundo.com

In the northern part of the county there are the **Carlsbad Premium Outlets**, featuring four block-like structures housing discount outlets from the likes of Calvin Klein, Barney's New York, and Donna Karan. Lots of restaurants onsite, too. *Info:* www.premiumoutlets.com

BEST NIGHTLIFE
San Diego used to have a reputation as a sleepy town, but not anymore. If you want to bar hop, park the car (and call a taxi afterwards if you have to) and stroll the **Gaslamp Quarter** (www.gaslamp.org) in between Broadway and Harbor Drive, and 4th to 6th Streets. Fifth Street has the most concentration of bars, lounges and pubs. Try **The Bitter End** or **Croce's** (owned by the wife of the late singer Jim Croce) or check out **Confidential** over on 4th, co-owned by Andrew Firestone of *The Bachelor* fame.

On weekends The **UBAR** at **Yard House**, located at 4th and Broadway, heats up after 10pm. If you're not in the mood for the bar scene, **Café Sevilla** hosts elaborate flamenco dinner shows complete with Spanish tapas and sangria.

Down at **Mission Beach** (www.sandiego.org), where college coeds dwell, it's a little more laid back and the dress code is mostly jeans and sandals. Popular beach-style bars and pubs include **The Sandbar Sports Grill**, **The Beachcomber**, and **The Wavehouse**. Neighboring **Pacific Beach** (www.sandiego.org) has more of the same — coeds, flip-flops and beach bars — but a swanky place has moved into this surf ghetto. The **Tower Bar** at Tower 23 Hotel attracts a very upscale crowd to its indoor/outdoor venue. It's all about sipping cosmopolitans, nibbling sushi, and lookin' good.

BEST SPORTS & RECREATION
Pro Baseball
The new **PETCO Park** is absolutely one of the best settings to watch baseball and is home to the beloved **San Diego Padres**. Located in the South Embarcadero area of downtown, sometimes referred to as the East Village, just a few blocks from the Gaslamp Quarter and harbor, the stadium features 42,000

fixed seats that are angled towards the infield. The historic Western Metal Supply Company building, a relic from decades past, was incorporated into the ballpark's design. The Padres play April through October. *Info:*www.sandiego.padres.mlb.com.

Pro Football
Take in a **San Diego Chargers** game at Qualcomm Stadium (formerly Jack Murphy Stadium) in Mission Valley September through December. *Info:* www.chargers.com.

Horse Racing
Del Mar Race Track is where the turf meets the surf every summer. Founded by Bing Crosby, Pat O'Brien and Jimmy Durante in the 1930s, this lovely course and its Spanish-style grandstand is open to the King of Sports late July to early September. *Info:*www.dmtc.com.

Golf
Your hotel concierge should be able to assist you with tee times at any one of the local courses. Some resorts only allow their guests to golf on their courses, but that's not the case at the Arnold Palmer-designed **Aviara Golf Club** at the Four Seasons Aviara Resort (www.fourseasons.com/aviara) in Carlsbad. One of the most spectacular public courses is **Torrey Pines Municipal Golf Course** (www.torreypinesgolfcourse.com) in La Jolla with a pair of 18-hole courses overlooking the ocean.

The **Coronado Municipal Golf Course** (www.golfsd.com/coronado) on Coronado Island is an 18-hole public golf course with the Glorietta Bay Marina, San Diego-Coronado Bridge and the Hotel Del Coronado as a backdrop. Bill Clinton shot a 79 here. The cost is only $13 during twilight tee times.

Tennis
Most hotels and resorts in San Diego feature tennis courts. The **Balboa Tennis Club** (www.balboatennis.com), located in Balboa Park near the world-famous San Diego Zoo, has 25 hard courts, 19-lighted courts plus a 2,000-seat stadium for professional tournaments. **Coronado Island** (www.coronado.ca.us) also has municipal courts located at Sixth Street and D Avenue; at Glorietta

Boulevard at Pomona Avenue; and on Coronado Cays Boulevard near the fire station.

Hiking

San Diego has one of the wildest stretches of land along the coast – **Torrey Pines State Reserve** (www.torreypine.org). Located in La Jolla near the Lodge at Torrey Pines (see San Diego Best Sleeps), this 2,000-acre sprawl features eight miles of trails, a visitors center, and guided nature walks on weekends and holidays. There are miles of unspoiled beaches, a lagoon that is home to migrating seabirds, and lots of photo opportunities. North of Torrey Pines State Reserve, in the city of Carlsbad, is the **Batiquitos Lagoon** (www.batiquitosfoundation.org), one of the few remaining coastal wetlands in the state. The long and varied hiking trail reveals an array of wildlife and plants.

Surfing

With all that coastline and spectacular beaches, San Diego has some great surfing spots. Committed surfers head to **Trestles** on the Orange County border. It's a long hike from the parking lot to the surf, but it's a popular destination for long board veterans. **Swami's**, named for the Self Realization Fellowship complex that sits high above on the bluff, is located in Carlsbad and is popular because of its ex-

tra swell energy. The beach in **Del Mar** is expansive, so you'll see a lot of surfers spread out waiting to catch the next big wave. However, the best surfing is **Black's Beach** in La Jolla.

School of Surf!

Learn to surf at either **San Diego Surfing Academy** (www.surfingacademy.com) or the **Surf Diva Surf School** (www.surfdiva.com), the number one surf school for girls and women.

Walking & Biking

San Diego is really about enjoying the great outdoors, so hop on a bike or put your two-legs to work with a walk along downtown's **Embarcadero Boardwalk** running along the harbor. **Mission Beach** and **Pacific Beach** also have great

great seaside boardwalks for bike riding. You can rent a **Surrey Cycle** (www.wheelfunrentals.com), which holds 2-4 people, and cruise in style.

Day Spas
You're going to find the most plush day spas at the best resorts. Among the crème de la crème are:
- **The Spa at La Costa** (www.lacosta.com) in Carlsbad
- **The Spa at The Del** (www.hoteldel.com) on Coronado Island
- **Spa at Rancho Valencia Resort** (www.ranchovalencia.com) in Rancho Santa Fe

ORANGE COUNTY

BEST SHOPPING
Shopping is an art form in Orange County, and there are two premier destinations for this favorite pastime. **South Coast Plaza**, located at Bristol Avenue and the 405 Freeway in Santa Ana on the Costa Mesa border, contains every major department store (Nordstrom and Bloomingdale's among them), national retailers, specialty store, and high-end designers. The complex is made up of two separate buildings connected by the covered Bridge of the Gardens. The main building, the larger of the two, houses several wings on two levels, while the neighboring annex across the street is mostly dedicated to home furnishings. There are lots of dining options, from casual to very upscale, though there is no central food court. Across the street on the other side is **South Coast Village**, also part of the complex, featuring just a handful of shops, some renowned restaurants, and a movie theater. *Info:* www.southcoastplaza.com.

Down the road a bit in tony Newport Beach is **Fashion Island**, often used as a backdrop in the now defunct TV series *The OC*. This open-air marketplace, punctuated by fountains, a koi pond and lush landscaping, is close to the ocean and also features a number of upscale shops, boutiques and restaurants. There are several spokes to explore, and it's rather easy to get turned around as you wander past Bloomingdale's, Neiman Marcus and other high-end shops. The indoor atrium, a three-level rotunda, houses many of the home stores, such as Restoration Hardware and Bloomingdale's Home Store. A food court, featuring a mix of cuisine, is located on the lower level. There are several restaurants located throughout the center, as well as on freestanding pads surrounding Fashion Island. Carousel and train rides will run you a buck each per child. *Info:* shopfashionisland.com.

Orange County

The **Irvine Spectrum**, inspired by the world-famous Alhambra, the 13th century citadel overlooking Granada, Spain, is another inviting outdoor center. Located where the 5 and 405 Freeways meet, just a bit inland from Laguna Beach and a few miles down the road from South Coast Plaza, the center is home  to Nordstrom and Target, and lots of restaurants, including Yard House and Cheesecake Factory. The Irvine Spectrum also boasts a giant Ferris wheel, lots of fountains and pathways, and several unique retailers. *Info:* www.shopirvinespectrum.com.

If you want to stay clear of the mall, you may want to shop the villages of either **Corona del Mar** or **Laguna Beach**, both just minutes from Fashion Island. Corona del Mar is actually part of Newport Beach, but it has the feel of being its own town. The retail district begins at MacArthur Boulevard, and on either side of Pacific Coast Highway there are plenty of shops and cafes. Further down the road heading towards Laguna Beach is **Crystal Cove Promenade** featuring a number of specialty stores including Williams-Sonoma, Banana Republic, The Gap and 14 other stores and restaurants. *Info:* www.visitnewportbeach.com.

Continuing along Pacific Coast Highway, you'll arrive to the town of **Laguna Beach**. Most of the shopping and art galleries are located in the heart of the village along Pacific Coast Highway, Broadway, Forest Avenue and Glenyere. Places you may want to visit are **Fiori**, specializing in fine Italian and Greek Majolica

Orange County

dinnerware and accessories, and **Sherwood Gallery** for its unconventional approach to art. *Info:* www.lagunabeachinfo.com.

BEST NIGHTLIFE
Sutra Lounge (sutralounge.com) atop Triangle Square in Costa Mesa is *the* place to go for dancing and meeting people. It gets crowded, so arrive early. If you want a more casual, but still upscale crowd, go next door to **Yard House** (www.yardhouse.com). This restaurant has an island bar with 200 taps of beer, a long list of martinis, and a late-night menu. No dancing, but still very social and happening.

The beach cities all have a rather healthy nightlife, though more subdued than what you'd find in Los Angeles or downtown San Diego. Main Street in **Huntington Beach** has a lot of pubs, bars and lounges that attract a young, surfer crowd. Start at Pacific Coast Highway and work your way up Main with stops to **Hurricanes Bar & Grill**, The **Longboard Restaurant & Pub**, and **Fred's Mexican Café**. Down the road in **Corona del Mar** along Pacific Coast Highway there is **Bandera** and **The Quiet Woman**. For live music **Opah Restaurant and Bar** (www.opahrestaurant.com) at the Irvine Market Place has a very stylish bar with a clientele to match. Several nights a week live jazz and R&B are featured. **The Coach House** in San Juan Capistrano has been attracting

Best Oceanfront Bars

- **Duke's Place at The Balboa Bay Club & Resort**, www.balboabayclub.com. Tel. 714/645-5000. Newport Beach.
- **Las Brisas**, www.lasbrisaslagunabeach. Tel. 949/497-5434. Laguna Beach
- **The Lobby Lounge at Montage Resort & Spa**, www.montagelagunabeac.com. Tel. 949/715-6000. Laguna Beach
- **The Bar at the Ritz-Carlton Laguna Niguel**, www.ritzcarlton.com. Tel. 949/240-2000. Dana Point
- **Splashes Lounge at the Surf and Sand Resort**, www.surfandsandresort.com. Tel. 949/376-3779. Laguna Beach
- **Commodore's Bar & View Deck at the Laguna Cliffs Marriott**, www.lagunacliffs.com. Tel. 949/661-5000. Dana Point

music aficionados for decades (www.thecoachhouse.com). The club
showcases headlining performers as well as emerging artists.

BEST SPORTS & RECREATION
Pro Baseball
Change is always difficult. Last year a brou-ha-ha occurred when
the **Anaheim Angels** changed their name to the Los Angeles
Angels of Anaheim (kind of an oxymoron considering Anaheim is
not even in the same county as Los Angeles). The team plays at
Anaheim Stadium from April through October. *Info:*
www.losangeles.angels.mlb.com.

Pro Hockey
Orange County's only hockey team also underwent a name change,
but no one seemed to mind. The **Anaheim Ducks** (formerly the
Mighty Ducks), part of the National Hockey League, play at the
Honda Center (formerly the Arrowhead Pond of Anaheim) from
October through April. *Info:* www.mightyducks.com.

Horse Racing
Enjoy live quarter horse racing four nights a week—Thursday
through Sunday— all year long at **Los Alamitos Race Course** in Los
Alamitos. General admission is just $3. *Info:*www.losalamitos.com.

Golf
There are plenty of golf courses in Orange County, from the
beach to the furthest point inland. **Monarch Beach Golf Links**
(www.monarchbeachgolf.com) is located along the coast in Dana
Point, **Meadowlark Golf Course** (meadowlarkgc.com) is a few
miles inland in Huntington Beach, and **Coyote Hills Golf Course**
(coyotehillsgc.com), located in the northern part of the county, is
another option. Ask your hotel concierge for recommendations
or if the hotel has privileges at any local courses.

Tennis
Most of the hotels in Orange County have tennis courts, but many
of the public parks also have tennis courts that are free to the
public on a first come, first-served basis. Both the **Fountain**

Valley Tennis Center (Tel. 714/839-5950) and the **Irvine Tennis Association** (949/669-0734) are open to the public.

Hiking

One of the most interesting and diverse places to go for a hike is the **Bolsa Chica Ecological Reserve** in Huntington Beach. Owned

 by the California State Land Commission, the reserve extends along the east side of Pacific Coast Highway between Warner and Seapoint Avenues. This coastal wetlands is comprised of 330 acres and home to nearly 200 species of birds. The Bolsa Chica Land Trust offers free public tours of the wetlands and mesa area on the third Sunday of each month from 10am-noon. *Info:* www.surfcityevents.com.

Another option is **Crystal Cove State Park** between Corona del Mar and Laguna Beach. Encompassing 2,000 acres and stretching several miles along Pacific Coast Highway, the area is an undeveloped woodland ideal for hiking or mountain biking. The offshore waters are designated as an underwater park. *Info:* www.crystalcovestatepark.com.

Biking & Walking

It's unanimous: The **Huntington Beach Ocean Strand** is the best place to walk or bike ride in The OC. Stretching 8.5 miles, the paved pathway is a recreational boardwalk that runs the entire length of the city. Along for the ride are skateboarders, roller skaters and moms pushing strollers. *Info:* www.surfcityusa.com.

Surfing

You can surf at most every Orange County beach, but some, because of their geographical position, have better surf than others. **Huntington City Beach** (www.surfcityusa.com), located at the foot of Main Street near the pier, is where the US Open of Surfing takes place each year. It's also where the USA Surf Team undergoes rigorous training to prepare for its many international competitions. Local surfers congregate here daily. If you're a novice or just learning to surf, **Doheny State Beach** in Dana Point is the ideal spot, especially for long boarders. Seal Beach, Newport Beach, and Laguna Beach are also ideal for surfing.

Want to ride a wave like a pro? There are several **surfing schools** located in Orange County, including **Newport Surf School** (www.newportsurfschool.com) and **Soul Surfing School** (www.soulsurfingschool.com). Both offer private and group lessons.

Day Spas
Without a doubt, the best spas in Orange County are located at the coastal resorts. **Pacific Waters Spa** (www.pacificwatersspa.com, pictured right) is located in the Hyatt Regency Huntington Beach Resort and Spa and offers a fabulous setting and long list of signature treatments. Then there is **Spa Montage** (www.spamontage.com) at the  Montage Resort & Spa in Laguna Beach, located oceanfront. And, finally, the **Spa at Laguna Cliffs** inside the Laguna Cliffs Marriott Resort & Spa (www.lagunacliffs.com) in Dana Point offers 14,000 square feet of total relaxation.

SANTA BARBARA

BEST SHOPPING
You'll quickly learn after arriving in Santa Barbara that lower **State Street**, from the Cabrillo Avenue at the beach to Sola several blocks north, is the hub of Santa Barbara living. Here is where you'll find block after block of great shopping, as well as charming outdoor cafes, restaurants and coffeehouses. There are a number of hidden courtyards and arcades revealing more boutiques, including **Victoria Court, La Arcada Court** and historic **El Paseo,** California's very fist shopping center dating back to the 1920s. *Info:* www.santabarbaradowntown.com.

Along State Street is also **Paseo Nuevo**, which is about 15 years old but looks like it very much belongs with the original State

Street architecture. Yes, it's a mall, but it's very intimate with cobbled pathways, fountains and elevated passageways. There is a Nordstrom and Macy's, plus several small shops consisting of both national and individual retailers. *Info:* www.sbmall.com.

In Montecito, which is a very upscale village and home to throngs of celebrities, **Coast Village Road** offers a number of fine galleries, high-end boutiques, day spas, and home furnishing stores. Along the way are some wonderful restaurants and cafes. *Info:* www.coastvillage.com.

BEST NIGHTLIFE
To be perfectly honest, there isn't much of a nightlife in Santa Barbara. Weekdays the sidewalks roll up rather early. On Friday and Saturday nights, especially during the summer, the bars and lounges along State Street are busier. The **Longboard Bar** at the end of **Stearns Wharf** gets lively and the views from the outdoor deck are excellent. **Soho**, on State Street, is just one of a few places that has live music and dancing. Hotel bars, such as the **Andalusia** or the **Four Seasons Biltmore**, are elegant spots to enjoy an after-dinner drink.

If you're visiting in the summer there are two venues that shouldn't be missed. The **Music Academy of the West**, the "Julliard of the West Coast," hosts an annual outdoor summer concert series — mid June to mid August — attended by most of the town. The academy's young artists perform everything from baroque to classical music to new works. *Info:* www.musicacademy.org. Tel. 805/969-4726. Montecito. 1070 Fairway Road. The other venue is the lovely 4,000-seat **Santa Barbara Bowl**, which features headlining acts in a beautiful outdoor setting. Past performers have included everyone from Rod Stewart to Tony Bennett. Food and drink must be purchased inside the bowl. *Info:* www.sbbowl.com. Tel. 805/962-7411. East of Downtown. 1122 N. Milpas.

Wine Tasting
It used to be that Napa Valley was synonymous with California's Wine Country. But, thanks to the movie *Sideways*, Santa Barbara's wine trails are now fraught with would-be oenophiles in search of the perfect pinot noir. There are two major wine trails in the

Santa Ynez Valley — Foxen Canyon and Santa Ynez — with the hamlets of Los Olivos, Santa Ynez, Solvang, and Buellton serving as entry points. Most wineries charge for their tastings with some offering souvenir glasses or credit towards a purchase. Many wineries also have picnic areas where you can enjoy lunch and your new wine acquisition. *Info:* www.sbcountywines.com.

BEST SPORTS & RECREATION
Polo
There aren't many spectator sports to speak of in Santa Barbara, unless you want to cheer on the Gaucho basketball team at UC Santa Barbara. However, the **Santa Barbara Polo & Racquet Club**, located to the south in Carpinteria, opens its grounds to the public every Sunday from late spring to early fall at 1pm and 3pm for the weekly polo matches. Tickets are just $10 per person. *Info:* www.sbpolo.com.

Golf
Santa Barbara and its surrounding neighborhoods offer some of the most breathtaking greens. But wind conditions can be almost as challenging as the courses themselves. Area pros suggest you estimate the wind's velocity before you choose your course. Your hotel concierge can help select and arrange tee times for you. Some courses you might want to consider are the **Santa Barbara Municipal Golf Course**, the **Rancho San Marcos Golf Course** de-

signed by Robert Trent Jones, the seaside **Sandpiper Golf Course** to the north in Goleta (pictured above); and the **River Course at the Alisal** in Solvang. *Info:* www.santabarbaraca.com.

Surfing
The best beaches for surfing are **Goleta Beach Park**, just north of Santa Barbara; SB's **Leadbetter Beach**; and **Rincon Beach** near Carpinteria. *Info:* www.santabaraca.com.

Tennis

The larger resorts, such as **Fess Parkers DoubleTree Resort,** have tennis courts for guests' use, but much of Santa Barbara's lodging consists of small and boutique hotels that don't have this amenity. There are public courts throughout town, including **Los Positas Courts** (Tel. 805/564-5418), **Oak Park** (Tel. 805/564-5517), and **Pershing Park Courts** (Tel. 805/564-5418).

Hiking

At the base of the **Santa Ynez Mountains** in Goleta you'll find some excellent foothill trails ideal for day hikes. General maps and information can be obtained from the **Los Padres National Forest.** *Info:* www.fs.fed.us/r5/lospadres. Tel. 805/683-6711. Both Borders Books and Music, along with Barnes and Noble, are located on State Street and have a local travel section where you can obtain maps.

Horseback Riding

Goleta, north of Santa Barbara, has two places where you can rent horses. **Circle Bar B Guest Ranch** (www.circlebarb.com) offers 90-minute excursions through the backwoods of Refugio Canyon or half-day rides which include a picnic lunch. **Rancho Oso Riding Stables** (www.rancho-oso.com) also offers one-hour horseback rides.

Biking & Walking

The **Bike Path**, which runs from the Andree Clark Bird Refuge all the way to Leadbetter Beach and contines out towards to UC Santa Barbara, is full of people walking, cycling and skating. You can rent Surrey Cycles and other types of non-motorized vehicles from **Wheel Fun Rentals** (www.wheelfunrentals.com) with locations at 101 State Street and at **Fess Parker's DoubleTree Hotel** along the waterfront (*see Santa Barbara Best Sleeps*). You may also find strolling through Santa Barbara's residential neighborhoods, east of State Street above Sola, to be enjoyable. The roads near the mission are filled with lovely homes.

Day Spas

Wine tasting and day spas seem like a good pairing. Perhaps that's why there are so many places in Santa Barbara to enjoy both. Of course, the best spas are found at the major resorts, and innkeepers at some of the boutique properties will make arrangements for treatments en suite. However, Santa Barbara has a few good day spas, including **Camille** in downtown Santa Barbara (Tel. 805/899-4883) and **Sea Spa** in Montecito (Tel. 805/565-5555).

PALM SPRINGS

BEST SHOPPING
There are a few malls in the area, but they're nothing special. Instead, head to **The Gardens** on **El Paseo** where you'll find two open-air levels anchored by Saks Fifth Avenue and Tiffany and filled with both national and independent retailers. *Info:* www.thegardensonelpaseo.com.

Desert Hills Premium Outlets also has designer wares, but at a fraction of the cost. Located in Cabazon, about 20 minutes from Palm Springs, be prepared to spend a good chunk of the day browsing this enormous, outdoor complex with more than 100 stores. *Info:* www.premiumoutlets.com.

BEST NIGHTLIFE
Palm Springs and the desert resort communities have a subdued nightlife. You may find your hotel bar your best bet for a drink and, maybe, live music. **The Nest** in Indian Wells has a friendly piano bar and gets its share of celebrities passing through. *Info:* www.gotothenest.com.

There are a handful of Indian casinos in the area, including **Agua Caliente Casino** (www.hotwatercasino.com) in Rancho Mirage, **Fantasy Springs Resort Casino** (www.fantasyspringsresort.com) in Indio, and **Spa Resort Casino** (www.sparesortcasino.com) in downtown Palm Springs, which offer gaming opportunities and live lounge acts.

Palm Springs is a favorite escape for **gay and lesbian travelers** wth many hotels and inns catering exclusively to this niche market.

Palm Springs

From historic inns to clothing-optional boutique resorts, gay and lesbian travelers have their pick. A few to consider are:
* **Avalon Private Resort**, Tel. 760/322-2404
* **Camp Palm Springs**, Tel. 760/320-5984
* **Chaps Inn**, Tel. 769/327-8222
* **Queen of Hearts Resort**, Tel. 760/322-5793

BEST SPORTS & RECREATION

For a truly memorable experience, take a sunrise or sunset hot-air balloon ride above the desert. **Balloon Above the Desert** is one company that offers this service. *Info:* Tel. 760/776-5785. You can also tempt fate with **Parachutes Over Palm Springs**, a 35-second free fall experience followed by a five-minute parachute ride to the desert floor. *Info:* Tel. 760/345-8321.

Golf

There are more than 100 courses within the desert resort communities, and the best are located at the area's top resorts. **La Quinta Resort and Club** (www.laquintaresort.com) has five championship courses, **The Westin Mission Hills Resort** (www.westinmissionhills.com) is home to courses designed by Pete Dye and Gary Player, and the 27-hole Ted Robinson-designed course at **Rancho Las Palmas Resort & Spa** (www.rancholaspalmas.com) is yet another option.

Tennis

All the big resorts have their own tennis courts and clubs, and I would say if that's what you're in town for then stay at **La Quinta Resort & Club**. It's got one of the best tennis clubs in the desert with 18 hard courts and five clay courts. It's only open to resort guests and club members. If you're not staying at a resort with tennis courts, I recommend the **Palm Desert Resort Country Club**. *Info:* www.theresorter.com.

Hiking

Palm Springs and the surrounding area offers a web of hiking trails through the scenic desert and neighboring mountain ranges. Top picks, both of which are covered in the *Palm Springs* chapter, include **Indian Canyons** and **Joshua Tree National Park**. Another top hiking location is the **Mt. San Jacinto Wilderness State**

Park, located in the San Bernardino National Forest. For a day permit to the latter, call the Ranger Station. *Info:* Tel. 760/325-1391.

Horseback Riding

Smoke Tree Stables, part of Smoke Tree Ranch, offers horseback rides through the Indian Canyons. Special add-ons include all-day rides with lunch as well as Western outdoor cookouts. *Info:* Tel. 760/327-1372.

Day Spas

You can't go wrong booking a spa treatment at anyone of the major resorts. The treatments and settings at **Well Spa at the Miramonte Resort, Spa Esmeralda at the Renaissance Esmeralda Spa and Resort**, and **Spa La Quinta at La Quinta Resort & Club** rank among the best. All are listed in the *Best Sleeps & Eats Chapter*.

11. PRACTICAL MATTERS

GETTING TO SOUTHERN CALIFORNIA

Airports/Arrivals
Southern California is served by four major airports, as well as by a handful of regional airports. There are taxis, shuttle services, hotel courtesy vans, and public buses located at all the airport terminals as you exit the baggage claim area – in most cases there are marked signs where these vehicles are allowed to stop. Except for Los Angeles International Airport (LAX) and San Diego International Airport (SAN), all of the other airports serving Southern California have **car rental companies** located on-site. LAX and SAN have several off-site rental car companies that are allowed to pick up and drop off their guests directly from the airline terminals using courtesy shuttle vans.

Greater Los Angeles is served by **Los Angeles International Airport** (LAX), the world's fifth busiest passenger airport, which is home to more than 90 national and international airline carriers. This is the closest major airport to **Santa Barbara**, and LAX is also the number one international gateway to Asia/Pacific. **Ontario International Airport** (ONT), a medium hub, full-service airport, also serves the Greater Los Angeles area to the east. ONT would be the logical choice if you're main destination is the Palm Springs and the dessert resort communities. Both LAX and ONT are part of Los Angeles World Airports (LAWA). *Info:* www.lawa.org.

There are also **two regional airports** serving the Los Angeles area and if you can get a non-stop flight from your hometown into either one, I highly recommend that you do.

Long Beach Airport (LGB), situated midway between Los Angeles and Orange County, is known as the region's "Easy In, Easy Out" airport. *Info:* www.longbeach.gov/airport. Tel. 562/570-2628. Long Beach. 4100 Donald Douglas Drive.

Burbank Airport (BUR) recently underwent a name change to **Bob Hope Airport**, but people still refer to it by its former name. It is the closest airport to downtown Los Angeles, Hollywood, the San Fernando Valley and Pasadena areas. You can also fly into Bob Hope Airport if your first stop is Santa Barbara. *Info:* www.burbankairport.com, Tel. 818/840-8840. Burbank. 2627 North Hollywood Way.

If you plan on spending most of your time in the **San Diego** area, then you'll want to fly into **San Diego International Airport** (SAN), also known as Lindbergh Field, located three miles from downtown. This is the county's only commercial airport. *Info:* www.san.org/airport, Tel. 619/400.2400. San Diego. 3225 North Harbor Drive.

John Wayne Airport (SNA), the 15th busiest airport in the world for takeoffs and landings, serves Orange County. The airport is located in Santa Ana off the 405 Freeway near the cities of Irvine, Costa Mesa and Newport Beach. It is 11 miles from Anaheim/ Disneyland area and 35 miles south of Los Angeles. This is the county's only commercial airport, but you can also conveniently fly into **Long Beach Airport** (Los Angeles County) if you're starting your trip in Orange County. *Info:* www.ocair.com. Tel. 949/252-5200. Santa Ana. 18601 Airport Way.

Palm Springs was recently a regional airport, but its growing status resulted in a name change to **Palm Springs International Airport**. *Info:* www.palmspringsairport.com. Tel. 760/318-3800. Palm Springs. 3400 East Tahquitz.

Santa Barbara Airport (SBA), located north of town, features non-stop service to and from Dallas/Ft. Worth, Denver, Las Vegas, Los Angeles, Phoenix, Portland, Salt Lake City, San Francisco, San Jose, and Seattle. *Info:* www.flysba.com. Tel. 805/681-4804. Santa Barbara. 500 Fowler Road.

GETTING AROUND SOUTHERN CALIFORNIA

By Air

You can city hop by air through Southern California, though **I don't recommend it**. The furthest point, from San Diego proper to Santa Barbara proper (there are no direct flights between the two cities), follows the coast for a good chunk of the way and will only take you four hours by car without traffic. If along the way you feel inclined to make pit stops to various attractions, or just take in the scenery from behind the wheel, you have that option.

Another reason I don't recommend inter-city air travel in Southern California is because of the hassle in our post 9/11 world. It will rarely save you time as all airlines require you to check in at least two hours prior to your flight and, depending on where you are departing from and arriving to, it's very likely you'll encounter freeway congestion (allow for travel time to the airport), airport congestion, long lines at the check-in counter, security checks, a wait at baggage claim, and possible delays in taking off and/or landing. By the time you add all of these factors into the mix, you could have likely reached your destination while the plane is still en route.

By Bus

Greyhound provides inter-city bus service throughout Southern California. The one unique trait about going Greyhound is that the bus often travels the back roads, stopping in the smaller communities en route to the big cities. The downside is that it takes much longer to reach your destination. *Info:* www.greyhound.com. Tel. 800/231-2222.

By Car

The best and most convenient way to travel Southern California is by car. It's a sprawling region, and without a car it's likely you won't be able to take advantage of all there is to do and see. If you're not accustomed to heavy traffic conditions, five-lane highways and brisk speeds of up to 65 miles per hour or more, it may feel a bit intimidating at first. Once you get the hang of the freeway system, you'll be free to explore the region when and where you like.

Road maps of Southern California are available from AAA and at the desks of most car rental companies. Many rental car agencies also offer Global Positioning Systems (GPS) at an additional charge.

By Train

Train travel in Southern California can be very scenic. **Amtrak** has various routes that run through the region and state. The **Pacific Surfliner**, which hugs the coast for most of the way, travels from downtown San Diego to the heart of Santa Barbara with stops along the way, including four Orange County stops as well as a stop in downtown Los Angeles at Union Station. The **Coast Starlight** travels between Los Angeles (Union Station) and Santa Barbara before heading up the coast to its final destination in  Seattle. Finally, you can take the **Sunset Limited**, which concludes its route in Orlando, Florida, from Los Angeles (Union Station) to Palm Springs. *Info:* www.amtrak.com. Tel. 800/872-7245.

By Taxi

You usually will not have a problem hailing a cab in downtown LA or downtown San Diego. Taxis cruise the major hotels and entertainment venues. They are harder to come by in Orange County, but service is available. Have your hotel concierge or restaurant host call ahead for you. Palm Springs and Santa Barbara both have taxi service but, again, service is limited. If you can't find a taxi, have the hotel or restaurant call for you.

Public Transportation

Each city, except Palm Springs, has its own public transportation system which, depending on the city or town, includes buses, shuttles, light rail systems, trolleys, and other modes of transportation. Contact the following for routes, timetables and general information:

- **Los Angeles County Metropolitan Transportation Authority**, www.mta.net. Tel. 800/266-6883
- **San Diego Metropolitan Transit System**, www.sdcommute.com. Tel. 619/238-0100
- **Orange County Transportation Authority**, www.octa.net. Tel. 714/560-6282
- **Santa Barbara Metropolitan Transit District**, www.sbmtd.gov. Tel. 805/683-3702

Freeways

Southern California's **freeway system**, especially in Los Angeles County, can be a confusing web of merging lanes, on and off ramps, and fast-moving cars. Learning the freeway system can be somewhat challenging. First rule of thumb is that it's important to know that all freeways have both a name and number. The name should indicate the road's final destination, but this is not always the case. The San Diego Freeway, also known as the 405, doesn't end in San Diego but rather merges with the Interstate 5 Freeway in Orange County, also known as the Santa Ana Freeway. It is the 5 Freeway—the *Santa Ana Freeway*—that actually takes you to San Diego. Confusing, I know. There are many examples where the rule just doesn't apply, so you may want to refer to the freeway number and name chart on the next page.

Freeway Driving Tips

- **Call boxes** are located every quarter mile on the freeway, and operators can connect you to the Auto Club, family members or your insurance company. Face traffic, and be aware of on-coming vehicles.
- **Carpool lanes**, usually marked with a diamond symbol, and **metered on-ramps** are generally open to any vehicle with more than a solo driver. Pay attention, as there are a few exceptions.

Freeway Numbers & Names

Number	Name
2	Glendale
22	Garden Grove
71	Corona Expressway
105	Glen Anderson
170	Hollywood
710	Long Beach
14	Antelope Valley
60	Pomona
101	Ventura/Hollywood
134	Ventura
605	San Gabriel
10	Santa Monica/San Bernadino
57	Orange
91	Riverside/Artesia
118	Simi Valley/San Fernando Valley
405	San Diego
5	Golden State/Santa Ana
90	Marina
110	Pasadena/Harbor
210	Foothill

BASIC INFORMATION

Business Hours
These hours vary greatly depending on how you define "business." Services, such as dry cleaners and automotive repair shops, generally operate a standard 9-to-5 day Monday-Saturday. Retail stores and shopping malls are generally open seven days a week 10am-9pm Monday-Friday, until 7pm on Saturday, and from 11am-6pm on Sunday. Many major grocery stores and pharmacy chains, such as CVB, Walgreens and Rite-Aid, are open 24 hours. Cultural venues, such as museums, are often closed Monday and Tuesday so call ahead for hours.

Climate & Weather

Have you ever awoken on New Year's morning with the TV tuned to the Tournament of Roses Parade? The skies are blue, the sun is shining, and the spectators are in jeans, t-shirts and lightweight jackets. I can't lie: The weather in Southern California is unbeatable and there really is never a bad time to visit.

Along the ocean and the coastal regions, the weather boasts a **Mediterranean climate year-round**. Temperatures rarely drop below 40 degrees in the winter and seldom climb much above the 80-degree mark in the summer. As a result many of the hotels in the coastal towns, such as Santa Barbara, are not equipped with air conditioners. A thick **marine layer**, or fog, often hangs over the beach cities in the mornings and usually burns off by the early afternoon. While it creates plenty of bad hair days for its residents, it also serves as a natural cooling device and form of insulation. You'll discover the hottest months to be August and September with average temperatures ranging from the mid-70s to low 80s. Move a bit inland, and the temperatures begin to slightly rise. In fact, the Los Angeles valley areas can often be 10 degrees hotter than the coastal communities and, because mountains surround them, they are conducive to smog. December and January are the chilliest months when temperatures tend to fluctuate in the 50s.

The climate is typically dry, but an occasional swell of humidity can take place in the summer and torrid downpours can occur during the winter. Palm Springs on the other hand is scorching hot in the summer with temperatures often climbing into the triple digits – great hotel bargains to be found. The best time to visit Palm Springs, as hotel prices will indicate, is between October and May.

Electricity

The standard electrical current for Southern California, as well as the entire U.S., is 110 volts.

Emergencies & Safety

In life-threatening situations, emergency assistance for police, fire or medical needs is 911, which is a toll-free telephone call from any public phone. You may be required to dial a "9" first from a hotel room, or you can press zero and ask the hotel operator to assist you.

Be sure to take precautions as you would anywhere else. Don't leave expensive electronic devices or handbags on the front seat of your car, and lock your car when you enter and exit your vehicle. One precaution I always use as a hotel guest is to hang the "do not disturb" sign on the outside of my door once my room has been serviced and I'm leaving for the day. It makes it appear as if someone is in the room. Another safety precaution is to never open your hotel room door without first looking through the peephole.

Festivals & Holidays
Southern California, like the rest of the state, observes all national holidays. Some notable events that take place throughout the year are listed below:

January-February
Tournament of Roses Parade in Pasadena on New Year's Day; **Palm Springs International Film Festival** in mid-January; **Chinese New Year Parade** in LA's Chinatown (Downtown) February; the annual **Academy Awards** at the Kodak Theater in Hollywood in late February.

March-April
LA Marathon in March; **Return of the Swallows at the Mission San Juan Capistrano** in late March; **Santa Barbara International Film Festival** also in March; **Toyota Grand Prix of Long Beach** in April; **Los Angeles Times Festival of Books** on the UCLA campus in April; **Santa Barbara County Vintner's Festival** also in April.

May-June
KIFM Jazz Festival in San Diego's Gaslamp Quarter in late May; **Del Mar Fair** in San Diego begins mid- June.

July-August
Sawdust Festival in Laguna Beach starts July and continues

through late August; **Orange County Fair** is held for two weeks in July; **Fourth of July** aboard the Queen Mary in Long Beach; **Bastille Day Celebration** in Santa Barbara on or near July 14th.

September-October
LA County Fair held two weeks in September; **San Diego Street Scene** in the Gaslamp Quarter in mid-September; the annual **West Hollywood Halloween Street Party** on October 31; month-long **Halloween Haunt at Knott's Berry Farm** in Orange County.

November-December
Doo Dah Parade in Pasadena the Saturday after Thanksgiving;

and various **Christmas Boat Parades** taking place in most every coastal community during the month of December.

Smoking
Smoking is prohibited on all public transportation vehicles, in all public transportation vehicles, in public buildings, as well as inside restaurants and bars. Smoking is also banned in public outdoor places as well, including public beaches. Definitely ask before you light up, and you must be 18 years old to purchase tobacco products.

Telephone/Area Codes
Nothing is more confusing than the area code system in Southern California. Because of the number of cell phones, fax machines and old-fashioned landlines, several new area codes have been implemented in recent years and more are likely to come. Los Angeles County has seven area codes, San Diego trails with just three, while Orange County has two (another split may occur within the next 12 months). Palm Springs and Santa Barbara proper both have just a single area code.

Time Zone
The entire state of California operates on **Pacific Standard Time** (Greenwich Mean Time minus eight hours) and trails three hours

behind the East Coast. Daylight Savings Time is observed, and you may obtain the correct local time by dialing 853-1212 regardless of the area code.

Tourist Information

The California Department of Tourism can supply you with information on the entire state as well as selected regions. You can obtain visitors' guides, brochures, maps, and special publications to help you better plan your trip. Much of this can be done online. You can get a better sense of Southern California by visiting the specific visitors bureaus of the cities profiled in this book – after all, they are the *best of* Southern California. *Info:*www.visitcalifornia.com, Tel. 877/CALIFORNIA.

The county/regional tourist boards are:
- **Anaheim/Orange County Visitor & Convention Bureau**, www.anaheimoc.org. Tel. 714/765-8888
- **LA Inc.,** The Convention & Visitors Bureau, www.lacvb.com. Tel. 213/236-2331
- **Palm Springs Desert Resorts Convention & Visitors Authority**, www.palmspringsusa.com. Tel. 760/770-9000
- **San Diego Convention & Visitors Bureau**, www.sandiego.org. Tel. 619/232-3101
- **Santa Barbara Convention & Visitors Bureau**, www.santabarbaraca.com. Tel. 805/966-9222

INDEX

Things Change!

Phone numbers, prices, addresses, quality of service – all change. If you come across any new information, let us know. No item is too small! Contact us at :

jopenroad@aol.com
or
www.openroadguides.com

TravelNotes

Open Road Publishing

Open Road has launched **a radical new concept in travel guides**: matching the time you *really* have for your vacation with the right amount of information you need for your perfect trip! No fluff, just the best things to do and see, the best places to stay and eat. Includes one-day, weekend, one-week and two-week trip ideas. Now what could be more perfect than that?

Best Of Guides

Open Road's Best of Las Vegas, $14.95
Open Road's Best of Arizona, $14.95
Open Road's Best of Southern California, $14.95
Open Road's Best of Costa Rica, $14.95
Open Road's Best of Honduras, $14.95
Open Road's Best of Belize, $14.95
Open Road's Best of Ireland, $14.95
Open Road's Best of Italy, $16.95
Open Road's Best of Paris, $12.95

Personal Paradise Guides

... finding your perfect place to stay!
Personal Paradise Caribbean, $14.95
Personal Paradise Florida, $14.95
Personal Paradise Hawaii, $14.95

Family Travel Guides

Open Road's Italy with Kids, $16.95
Open Road's Paris with Kids, $16.95
Open Road's Caribbean with Kids, $14.95
Open Road's London with Kids, $14.95
Open Road's New York City with Kids, $14.95
Open Road's Best National Parks With Kids, $14.95
Open Road's Washington, DC with Kids, $14.95
Open Road's Hawaii with Kids, $14.95

Order now at www.openroadguides.com